EXPOSITORY
OUTLINES

from

1 and 2
CORINTHIANS

by
Kingsley G. Rendell

LONDON
PICKERING & INGLIS LTD
1969

PICKERING & INGLIS LTD.
29 LUDGATE HILL, LONDON, E.C.4
26 BOTHWELL STREET, GLASGOW, C.2

Printed in Great Britain by Robert MacLehose and Co. Ltd.
University Press, Glasgow

To the memory of my parents,
whose Godly living and self sacrificing love
made it possible for me to become a preacher of the Word

Preface

This volume is not intended to be read as a book of sermons, nor indeed is it to be regarded as a collection of sermonettes. Rather it is designed as a compilation of sermon outlines to aid those preachers who are eager to exercise a systematic expository ministry. In his Warrack Lectures on preaching, 'Heralds of God', that contemporary prince of the Scottish pulpit Dr. James S. Stewart makes the following plea for expository preaching. 'This is one of the greatest needs of the hour . . . Congregations are sick of dissertations on problems, and essays on aspects of the religious situation: such sermons are not preaching at all. Men are not wanting to be told our poor views and arguments and ideals. They are emphatically wanting to be told what God has said and is saying in His Word. . . . Let the Bible speak its own message . . . this will deliver us from the peril of monotony. . . . The preacher who expounds the Bible has endless variety at his disposal.'

Those who have exercised a systematic expository ministry would readily witness to the fact that far from lessening the spiritual appetite of their people it has created a hunger for the Word of God, and has resulted in producing not only a scripturally intelligent congregation but also a church fired with an enthusiasm for evangelism. The preacher who is content to jump from scripture to scripture throughout his ministry, not only is to be found frequently moving from one charge to another, but produces 'butterfly' hearers, whose Christian faith and experience is founded merely upon the understanding and application of isolated texts, and these often, alas, completely divorced from their context.

The preacher who applies himself to the discipline of systematic expository preaching discovers the infinite variety of Biblical wisdom, and at the same time ministers to the varied needs of both his people and the community in which they live. He does not have to waste precious time puzzling as to what topic he shall pursue, or what text he shall choose, his task is to expound faithfully the passage which lies to his hand. Dr. Max Warren in his timely book, *The Day of the Preacher*, has emphatically declared that today is 'a Day of Opportunity for a revival of expository preaching'. He reminds us that 'the great tradition of Christian preaching may be said to be the practice of expounding the Bible'.

In this volume of expository outlines, the author has been brief. Quotations are rare and illustrative material deliberately limited. The object is to assist those who are eager to maintain a systematic ministry, without robbing them of their originality, or denying them the joy of preparation. It is felt that those who treat these outlines as a guide, and refrain from slavish adherence to them, will obtain the most benefit from them. They are offered to those engaged in the ministry of the Word, with the prayer that they may be blessed by God to His glory.

Paul's Corinthian Epistles

Our Bibles contain only two letters addressed to the church at Corinth but modern scholarship is of the opinion that Paul wrote at least four. Indeed some scholars would insist that there were originally five Corinthian letters. It seems that before he wrote the epistle we know as 1 Corinthians he wrote a letter rebuking the Corinthian church for its moral laxity. Some authorities believe that 2 Corinthians 6.14–7.1 is a portion of that first letter. The epistle we know as 1 Corinthians was written partly to correct a misunderstanding which arose from the first and partly to deal with the divisions of which he had heard.

In this letter the apostle ranges over a variety of subjects from incipient sectarianism (1.10–4.21) to the offering which was being made to the poor saints in Jerusalem (chap. 16). The wide variety of its contents make it an ideal letter for systematic exposition. There is no danger of the congregation becoming bored with the sameness of the subject. Indeed, almost every subject which is of interest to a modern congregation is to be found within 1 Corinthians.

Paul's second letter to Corinth (our 1 Corinthians) may not have achieved the desired result. Consequently the apostle visited the city himself only to find the strength of the opposition to him (2 Cor. 12.14; 13.1 ff.). On his return from Corinth he wrote a further letter employing Titus as its carrier. Scholars are not agreed as to whether any of this letter has survived. Some believe 2 Corinthians 10.1–13.10 may be a part of it. This epistle was successful it seems and when Paul learnt from Titus of its success he wrote yet another letter which in the main is our 2 Corinthians (1.1–9.15; 13.11–14).

For the expositor the critical issues are not particularly important; he is more concerned with the message and principles applicable to every age.

Summary of 1 Corinthians

THE ADDRESSEES

Corinth was a Roman colony, situated on the isthmus separating the Ionian from the Aegean seas. It was not only an important port but also a vital military centre, commanding the trade routes of Greece. It was infamous on account of the vices which characterised its social life. Not without reason, has it been called 'The Vanity Fair of the Roman Empire'. In spite of its commercial affluence, it was a city of strange contrasts, poverty and wealth being found in close proximity.

THE PURPOSE OF ITS WRITING

To deal with the divisions which had arisen within its membership, and rebuke its disorders.

THE TIME AND PLACE OF ITS WRITING

It was probably written in A.D. 55 or 56 from Ephesus.

AN ANALYSIS OF THE EPISTLE

I Salutation (1.1–9)

II The Divisions Within the Church (1.10–4.21)
  i. An appeal for unity (1.10–17), since
    (a) divisions rob the Christian of the fulness of salvation (1.1–2.16)
    (b) divisions destroy fellowship between Christians (3.1–10)
    (c) divisions are a denial of Christ as the sole foundation of the faith (3.11–23)

9

1 CORINTHIANS 1. 1–3

Saluting the Saints

Corinth, a prosperous port and business centre was situated in
southern Greece, some fifty miles directly west of Athens. The
church in this city had been established through the work of
Paul, on the occasion of his second missionary journey. (For
details see Acts 18.1–18.) The church appears to have grown
rapidly in its early days, converts having been made among Jews
as well as Gentiles (see 7.18). This letter was written in reply to a
missive Paul had received from the church in Corinth (see 7.1).
Before he answers their questions, and deals with the difficulties
facing the church in Corinth, he salutes the saints in the city. The

prefaces to Paul's epistles are always full of charm, and well repay our study. From these opening words we learn four things.

1. The Servant is *A DIVINE AMBASSADOR*

Paul was first and foremost God's servant. At times he prefaced his epistles with this self designation (see Rom., Phil., Tit.). This is why he was able to write with such authority. His critics denied his apostleship, saying that he was not one of the original twelve, and had no right to call himself an apostle. Paul confessed that he was not meet to be called an apostle, and was in fact 'the least of the apostles', but the fact of his apostleship was beyond doubt. He had seen the risen Christ on the Damascus road. That constituted his right to be an apostle.

There are two words here we must emphasise: 'called' and 'apostle'. You will notice that the phrase 'to be' is in italics and should be omitted. The omission of this phrase emphasises the word 'called'. The Greek word *kletos* implies status. Paul had responded to the Divine summons, and having been called, he was sent. Such is the meaning of the word apostle; it comes from the Greek verb 'to send'. Paul was called and sent. Our Lord's first word to His disciples was 'Come' (John 1.39). His final word was 'Go' (Matt. 28.19). It is so with us.

Notice also the phrase 'through the will of God'. It is not only God's desire that we should be His servants, it is God's power which brings us into His service. How can we then refuse to go out and represent Him as His ambassadors in the world?

2. The Church is *A DIVINE SOCIETY*

Notice it is 'the church of God', not the church of Corinth. The church is 'at Corinth'. That is its earthly environment, but it is a colony of heaven on earth. The church can never be merely a human organisation. It is born from above (see the story of its origin Acts 2.1–13). It must ever be a Divine organism. It is 'of God'. God is its Creator and Sustainer.

It is hardly surprising in view of this that Paul goes on to designate the Christians which compose the church in Corinth as 'them that are sanctified in Christ Jesus, called saints'. This

11

means set apart, as vessels in Old Testament times were set apart for the service of the sanctuary. They are set apart to God 'in' Christ Jesus, or as it may be translated, 'through' Christ Jesus, 'called' (again the words 'to be' should be omitted) 'saints' or 'holy'. 'Set apart, holy' – that is the force of these words. How necessary it was to remind these Corinthian Christians of this, in view of the wickedness of the city in which they lived. Because they were God's, they were to be Godlike.

Further we must notice how Paul reminds them that they are not an isolated colony of God, but part of the universal church, which owns Christ as its Lord. Sectarianism was developing in Corinth. The church was beginning to divide (see 1.11–13), but Christ cannot be made a sectarian name, He is the one Lord of the whole church. He is both 'theirs and ours'.

3. Grace and Peace are *DIVINE BLESSINGS*

The Greek salutation was 'grace', the Jewish was 'peace'. Both are ours from God and Christ. Grace is the root and peace is the fruit. Notice they come from the Father and the Son. Alas, so often God is presented solely as the God of wrath, the Son as love. There is no tension between Father and Son in the Godhead. Father and Son co-operate in bringing the blessings of grace and peace to us who so sorely need them.

I CORINTHIANS I. 4–9

Cause for Thanksgiving

This was to be primarily a letter of reproof, but before the apostle reproves, he praises God on their behalf. Indeed there is continual praise on his part: we must not miss the little word 'always'. If the Corinthian Christians themselves had been the reason for his praise this would not have been the case. Paul inserts the word 'always' because the word that immediately precedes it is 'God'. If we keep our eye on God's faithful mercies rather than on our oftimes faithless witness, then there will always be cause for persistent praise. We must notice the reason for Paul's praise.

1. There is *GRACE WHICH ENRICHES OUR LIVES* v. 4

It is grace which saves us. That in itself is reason enough for praise, but grace is not merely an act of forgiveness in the past, it must be the experience of the present. Christ is the embodiment of God's redeeming love, and consequently, just as Christ is our present possession, grace is a present experience. In the prologue to his Gospel John declares, 'Grace and truth came by Jesus Christ' (1.17) and further he adds 'Of his fulness have all we received, and grace for grace', or as it may be translated, 'grace upon grace', like the rollers of the sea which break incessantly upon the shore. Grace not only saves, it enriches. The word literally means 'made wealthy'. Yet, alas, how many Christians live lives which are spiritually bankrupt, because they are not drawing upon the free grace of God!

It is grace which brings with it WISDOM. The word translated 'utterance', is *logos*, the word John employs to describe the Saviour as the 'Word' or 'wisdom' of God. A little later in verse 25 Paul writes of the 'foolishness of God' being 'wiser than men'. How true that is! More wonderful still is the fact that Christ, 'the wisdom of God' (v. 24) is ours.

It is grace which brings us KNOWLEDGE. The word is *gnosis*, which gave the name to 'the Gnostics', sects which in the early days of the church claimed a secret knowledge of the faith. With wisdom must go knowledge. For the mountaineer and the pot-holer enthusiasm is not enough; indeed it can be positively dangerous without knowledge. There must not only be Divine wisdom through grace, there must also be knowledge of the faith we profess.

Further, it is grace which brings about an UNDENIABLE CONFIRMATION OF OUR PROFESSION (v. 6). When Paul refers to the testimony of Christ he means the testimony to Christ borne by the apostles. This is the responsibility of the church, namely, to demonstrate in life the truth of the gospel. It is grace alone which allows us to witness effectively to Christ.

2. There are *GIFTS WITH WHICH WE EFFECT OUR MINISTRY* v. 7

The intimate connection between grace and gift can be seen more clearly when we examine the two Greek words employed. The word for grace is *charis*, while that for 'gift' is *charism*. Obviously Paul is not writing about natural gifts, but special endowment for the ministry of the church in the pagan city of Corinth. Paul makes it clear in the verses which follow (v. 17 in particular) that he had purposely avoided the display of natural gifts, that men might appreciate the glory of the gospel rather than admire his qualities as an orator.

Paul points to the incentive in the employment of our gifts, namely the coming of Christ at His second advent (v. 7). The word he uses for coming is *apocalupsis*, which means 'unveiling' or 'revelation'. The word translated 'waiting' does not imply being passive, but rather actively expecting the final unveiling. In view of the Second Advent we must constantly employ the gifts we have received.

Paul goes further, pointing out that the use of gifts will bring its confirmation at the judgement bar of God. We shall be unimpeachable, for such is the force and meaning of the word unfortunately translated 'blameless' in the A.V.

3. There is a *GOD WHO IS THE GROUND OF OUR HOPE* v. 9

God has pledged Himself to those of us who are believers in Christ. He cannot do more than this. We are brought not merely into partnership with Christ, although this is true, but into a communion of which Christ is the Head. Notice that Paul refers to Him as Lord. How privileged we are that God has pledged himself to us! How blessed is our fellowship with God in Christ!

The Unity of the Church

Not only is the disunity within the church confusing to the non-Christian, it is a distressing state of affairs to the majority of Christians. Boldly we proclaim there is 'One Lord, one faith, one baptism', yet we sadly sing,

'with a scornful wonder
Men see her sore oppressed,
By schism rent asunder
By heresies distressed'.

Obviously God meant the church to be a fellowship of believers; sadly it has become a victim of faction. We cannot justify denominationalism on the ground that they are regiments fighting together in the same army, since alas, far too often they have been engaged in warfare with each other. We do not read that at Pentecost when the church was born, 'They all went their different ways as they thought fit' but 'all that believed were together and had all things common . . . they did eat their meat with gladness and singleness of heart. . . . And the multitude of them that believed were of one heart and of one soul' (Acts 2.44, 46; 4.32). Their unity was the secret of their power. No wonder we read, 'with great power gave the apostles witness' (Acts 4.33). Denominationalism had not yet come to Corinth, but it was well on the way. Already the young church was disturbed by incipient sectarianism, although it had not yet reached the point of schism. Cliques had formed around outstanding personalities such as Paul, Peter and Apollos, and one party had even employed the name of Christ as the clique label. We do well to notice how Paul deals with this distressing situation.

1. There is *AN APPEAL FOR UNITY* v. 10

Paul did not appeal to these Corinthians on the ground of his apostleship. He does not order them but pleads with them as brethren. As brethren they owned the same Father, belonged to the same family, were born of the same Holy Spirit, and were united to the same Lord. That is why he appeals to them 'by the Name of our Lord Jesus Christ', that is, by the 'authority' of the Lord Jesus Christ, since 'name' in scripture means authority. In the Old Testament to know a man's name was to have authority over him. In claiming the name of Peter, Paul and Apollos, they were forgetting the fact that Christ is head of the church.

Notice too, Paul appeals to them to 'speak the same thing'. That does not mean they are to be 'yes' men one to another. It means that they are to speak publicly in their witness to the city as one church. How vital that the church speak to the world as one voice. How often we publicly voice our confusion to the world to whom we witness!

Further, we notice that the apostle appeals to the Corinthian Christians to be 'perfectly joined together'. This literally means perfectly adjusted, so that they can move together as an intricate piece of mechanism moves together harmoniously. Where there is mal-adjustment there will be friction; hence our heated relationships one with another. 'Adjusted in the same mind' does not mean we must all think alike. The term 'mind' here, as in Phil. 2.5, means 'attitude of heart', 'lowliness of mind'. Where there is humility there is not likely to be friction. Adjusted too, in the same judgement. This does not mean judgement of others, but 'discernment', which involves appreciation of the others point of view.

2. There is *AN ACCUSATION OF DISUNITY* v. 11

Because Paul appealed to them as brethren, it did not mean that he was not cognisant of the disunity which existed in Corinth. If he had merely appealed for unity in a general way, little notice might have been taken of his words. Paul makes it clear that he is well aware of the serious nature of the divisions within the church. First he names the source of his information. The Greek is stronger than our English translation; it means a detailed account. Indeed, no one in Corinth could deny that a distressing condition existed. Paul could not be accused of listening to rumour.

The seriousness of the situation is brought out in the word translated 'contentions'. It means more than dissensions, since one can dissent without bitterness. Here there was bitterness.

16

It is when we come to this point we see how far we are removed from the love of Christ, which should characterise all our dealings with others.

3. There is *AN ARGUMENT IN FAVOUR OF UNITY* v. 13

There was argument in Corinth, but it was argument which brought about disunity. Now Paul employs argument in the cause of unity. In these verses he exposes the folly of their partisanship. Did they owe their salvation to a human instrument, Paul himself, Apollos, or Cephas? Only a few could claim to be baptised by Paul. Notice how Paul elevates Christ as central to their faith and experience. Where Christ is the rallying point there can be no danger of disunity. Disunity results where we allow other loyalties to come between us and him.

4. There is *AN AFFIRMATION OF MISSION IN THE CAUSE OF UNITY* v. 17

Paul is not decrying baptism here. The sentence might be translated, 'Christ sent me not so much to baptise as to preach the gospel'. The gospel is the one message which brings salvation. The gospel is the one message the church must proclaim. It may be over ritual we quarrel, but we are one when we proclaim the gospel in simplicity. Denominations refuse to worship together because their rituals are different, but they will unite in an evangelistic campaign. Notice that Paul modifies his statement emphasising the gospel in its simplicity. We are agreed as to its content and its saving force. We wrangle when we begin to philosophise over its implications.

The Word of the Cross

Division at Corinth had been brought about by 'words', or rival philosophies. There were those who gloried in their Gentile liberty, others in their Jewish birth: yet others in their Hellenic culture. There were some who claimed to be exclusively the Lord's people, thus making the name of Christ a party label. Into this chaos of words, Paul brings *The Word*, that is *The Redemptive Word of the Cross*, the very centre of the Christian revelation. It deserves our careful attention.

1. It is *THE TOUCHSTONE OF MEN'S DESTINY* v. 18

The word translated 'preaching' is more correctly translated 'word'. Unfortunately the A.V. has not indicated the tense clearly; it should read 'them that are perishing' and 'us which are being saved'. It is by the cross that we stand or fall. It is by the cross we are being judged. If it is foolishness to us as it was to the Greek, then we are perishing by reason of our attitude to it. If it is to us a demonstration of God's dynamic, then we are being saved. What does this word really mean to us? How do we rate it?

2. It is the *INSTRUMENT OF THE BELIEVER'S SALVATION* v. 21

By the foolishness of preaching the word of the Cross, men are saved. God seeks to persuade men by word. That is why Jesus was careful in the performance of his miracles. He never employed miracles to create faith, but always demanded faith as a basis for miracle. God finds His way to men's hearts by way of the ear. The Jews were ever looking for signs. They demanded a sign from Jesus, but Jesus refused signs. He made it clear the only sign would be His triumphant resurrection, and that was not their idea of a sign. The Greeks gloried in their philosophy or reasoning, but the word of the cross is a proclamation to be believed not an argument to be understood. There have been many theories of the atone-

18

ment, but thank God we are not asked to believe in theories of the atonement; we are asked to accept the fact of it by faith. Thus the Cross becomes the instrument of the believer's salvation.

3. It is the *WISDOM AND DYNAMIC OF GOD'S PERSON* v. 24

Paul here contrasts the wisdom of the world, so manifest in Greek philosophy, with God's own wisdom. The wisdom of the world is foolishness to God; indeed the foolishness of God is wiser than men. The world with its sin has inverted Divine values. What the world despises God uses. This is part of God's purpose to show man that He cannot save himself.

If God were to use man's wisdom then man would be tempted to think he can save himself, or at least partly save himself. Paul would have none of this. His constant emphasis was that salvation is wholly of God, as he makes abundantly clear in the two closing verses of the chapter.

I CORINTHIANS I. 30–31

The All Sufficiency of Christ

The root of the trouble at Corinth was largely self sufficiency. Carlyle said, 'The greatest of faults is to be conscious of none'. Like the Pharisee far too often we thank God we are not as others. There is too much of the Laodicean spirit within the church. We boast that we are 'rich, and increased with goods, and have need of nothing' (Rev. 3.17). Where there is self sufficiency there can be no spiritual hunger or thirst. There the sufficiency of Christ will never be realised. What is the answer to this problem? Paul leaves us in no doubt. He stresses four aspects of Christian life and experience.

1. *THE SOURCE OF THE CHRISTIAN'S LIFE*

Paul informed the Corinthian believers that they were 'of Him'.

This is the very opposite to the language of self sufficiency. Our salvation is wholly of God. We are elect of Him in eternity. We are born *anothen*, that is, 'from above'. The language of the unbeliever is that of self sufficiency, as voiced by the foolish farmer in the gospel record, 'I will pull down my barns, and build greater . . . and I will say to my soul, "Soul, thou hast much goods laid up for many years; take thine ease" ' (Luke 12.18, 19). That is the sad soliloquy of self sufficiency. That kind of man is self possessed, boasts that he is self made, and is unbearably self righteous. Self is the means and self is the end of that man's life. He sees no need of Christ because he feels no need of Christ.

The Christian should present a striking contrast to the unbeliever. The Christian has learned to regard self as the most subtle enemy of the Christian life. At Corinth they had taken their eyes off Christ and focused them upon themselves, particularly on those whom they looked upon as their organisational leaders. They prided themselves on their philosophies. We need constantly to remind ourselves that we are 'of Him'.

2. *THE SPHERE OF THE CHRISTIAN'S LIFE*

Paul then informs his readers of their exalted position 'in Christ'. Andrew Murray stressed that 'the whole Christian life depends upon the clear consciousness of our position in Christ'. It was a favourite theme of Paul's. It is the theme of his Epistle to the Ephesians. He delighted to remind his readers of their mystical union with Christ. It is an organic union; we are grafted into Christ. Before grafting can take place the tree has to be incised, the branch inserted, and the bark bound. Grafting is not a natural process; it requires the experienced hand of the gardener. Our union with Christ is not the result of human wisdom or religious exercises, but the work of the Spirit of God. Indeed, the whole Trinity is involved in this process. The Father is the husbandman, the Son is the vine and we are the branches. God by His Spirit unites us to Christ by placing us in Him. Christ's call to His disciples was 'Abide in me' (John 15.4). We can only live the abounding life as we abide in Him.

3. *THE SUFFICIENCY OF THE CHRISTIAN LIFE*

The question inevitably arises, 'How is Christ sufficient?' The answer is here. It is expressed in one word: 'wisdom'. And what follows, namely, 'righteousness, and sanctification, and redemption' constitute a definition of Divine wisdom. The A.V. does not make this as clear as it might. At Corinth they were seeking human wisdom. What they needed most of all was Divine wisdom. That is first and foremost righteousness, the knowledge of being right with God and our fellow men. By nature we are unrighteous, but when we come to Christ we are made righteous. Righteousness leads to sanctification, the knowledge that we are set apart for God, a knowledge which must be confirmed by holiness of life. Righteousness and sanctification means redemption. We might expect redemption to be first not last in order. Paul has in mind the whole redemptive process of God, that is, final as well as primal redemption. He was thinking eschatologically. If righteousness is imputed and sanctification indicated, redemption of the body as well as the soul is imperative.

4. *THE SATISFACTION OF THE CHRISTIAN LIFE*

For the Christian there is only one thing which can give real satisfaction, and that is bringing glory to the Lord. Unbelievers find or try to find their satisfaction in self achievement. The Christian finds his in the Lord. 'He that glorieth, let him glory in the Lord.'

I CORINTHIANS 2. 1–16

Preaching the Gospel

Unfortunately the church in Corinth presented the picture of a market place, where a group of cheap jacks clammer to sell their wares, each eager to outdo his fellows. Paul passes through the midst of the Corinthian sectaries, heedless of their partisan cries, holding aloft the cross of Christ. He did not visit Greece with oratory and rhetoric, though he was able to have done so, but rather nervously and in human weakness. Paul was a puny figure and seems to have suffered from some form of inferiority complex. No preacher should ever enter the pulpit relying upon his natural gifts. Every preacher of the Word must face men, conscious of his own weakness, yet trusting in the power of God.

1. *THE DETERMINATION OF THE APOSTLE*
v.2

This does not mean Paul was ignorant of Greek thought and learning. He makes that clear in his sermon at Athens (Acts 17.22–31). Nor does it mean that he was blind to the conditions which prevailed in the church at Corinth. He meant rather that he had no intention of being drawn into their divisions. In considering Paul's determination there are three features of it we must not miss.

(*a*) *It is centred in a Person – Jesus Christ.* Christianity is not the religion of law, nor is it essentially that of a book, but that of a person. Christianity is Christ. This is no meaningless truism. It is the expression of the very heart of Christianity. Luther said 'Christianity is the religion of the personal pronoun'. It involves a personal relationship with Christ.

(*b*) *It is concerned with His Passion – Jesus Christ and Him crucified.* Paul made no apologies for the cross, even though it was a scandal to the Jew, and foolishness to the Greek. He knew that it exposed the awful depravity of the human heart, but he knew too, that it was the one redemptive force which could radically change the heart of man. 'I have never got away from Christ and Him crucified, and I found that when people were gripped by this great evangelical doctrine I had no need to give them instruction about morality,' said David Brainerd.

(*c*) *It is confirmed by our Personal Experience.* Mark the word Paul uses, 'know'. It is pious to talk about the cross, but it is salvation to experience its truth in our lives. This was Paul's principal concern. 'I count all things but loss for the excellency of

22

the knowledge of Christ Jesus,' he wrote to the Philippians, '. . . that I may know Him, and the power of His resurrection, and the fellowship of His sufferings' (Phil. 3.8, 10).

2. THE DEMONSTRATION OF THE SPIRIT'S POWER v. 4

We can preach apart from the Holy Spirit. Sermons can be easily worked up, but the only really effective ones are those sent down from God. Preaching which merely tickles the ear, moves the emotions, or stimulates thought is in vain unless it awakens the conscience. Paul was not disparaging preaching, indeed in chapter 1 he emphasises that this was his primary task. Here he goes further, pointing out the kind of preaching that is required. All apostolic preaching was in the power of the Spirit of God.

In verse 5 Paul gives a cogent reason why preaching should be in the power of the Spirit. Those who are won by intellectual argument will not stand in the faith. Further, verse 6 suggests that without the operation of the Spirit in preaching there is no possibility of converts growing in grace. There is no possibility of perfection, which means maturity or full growth.

3. THE DISCERNMENT OF THE BELIEVER

The key verse of this section is verse 11. In verse 7, Paul writes of a 'mystery'. A mystery in the New Testament is something which has hitherto been hidden but now revealed. The wisdom of God had now been made manifest in Christ, but it was wisdom which even the wise and noble of the world did not recognise (such is the meaning of 'princes' in verse 6). It is through the Spirit alone, that we as believers are enabled to know the wonder of God's purposes for us (v. 9). Like alone can understand like. Only the Spirit of God can understand the things of God. Before we can become a connoisseur of music, we must have a love for music. Spiritual things are spiritually discerned. The spiritual is the highest plane on which we can live. From this vantage point we can look down on life. We are able to see the panorama of life and judge rightly, since we have the right perspective, or as Paul puts it in verse 16, 'we have the mind of Christ'. How vital it is that we become truly spiritual men and women!

Three Striking Metaphors

In the previous chapter Paul emphasises the importance of living upon the spiritual plane. Unfortunately the Corinthians were not spiritual but carnal, or fleshly. They were not really concerned with spiritual things. They were allowing their old unregenerate nature to control them. Here there was no possibility of spiritual growth leading to maturity. Their incipient sectarianism was evidence of their carnality (v. 5). The folly of their partisan spirit is brought out in verses 5 and 6. Paul, Apollos and for that matter any other preacher, is but a servant, an agent in the work of redemption. The work of God's servants is complementary not competitive (v. 6). The glory must ever go to God. The climax of the Apostle's argument is to be found in verse 9. Here he makes plain the part we play.

1. We are *LABOURERS* v. 9

Here is the truth of Christian Co-operation. The emphasis is upon the Divine, we are God's labourers. This was a point which needed emphasis at Corinth, where God was rapidly being lost sight of in the midst of their sectarian rivalries. God's labourers; it is an interesting thought.

(a) *It is certainly A Humbling Thought.* Whatever part we may play in the service of the kingdom, whether conspicuous or otherwise, we are no more than labourers. Some prefer to think of themselves as managing directors. There does not appear to have been a clearly defined ecclesiastical hierarchy in the apostolic period. The term 'minister' means 'servant', and the word *diaconos* translated 'deacon' really means an 'errand boy'.

(b) *It is also An Honouring Thought.* We are labourers, but let us not forget we are God's fellow labourers. God has called us to be His fellows. There are legions of angels ready to do God's bidding, but the wonder of it is that in spreading the news of redemption God chooses those who have been redeemed.

2. We are *HUSBANDRY* v. 9

Again the apostle emphasises that we are God's husbandry. It means a cultivated field. It may seem a very odd metaphor to use, but it is certainly a very suggestive one.

(*a*) It implies *Separation*. Before a piece of land can be tilled, it has to be fenced. It has to be separated from the surrounding wilderness or common. This was the first step in the agriculture revolution of the eighteenth century; the movement known as 'enclosures'. This is what God does: He separates us to Himself.

(*b*) It also implies *Preparation*. Once the land has been enclosed it has to be cleaned and dug. This is the subjective work of the Spirit of God, constantly taking place.

(*c*) Further it means *Dissemination*. When the soil is ready the seed has to be sown. It raises the question, 'Are we fruitful or fallow?'

3. We are a *BUILDING* v. 9

The thought here is Construction. Paul refers to the body as a tabernacle, or temporary building. In verse 16 we have the words 'Know ye not that ye are the temple of God'. See also Eph. 2.21; 1 Pet. 2.5. What kind of tenants are we?

1 CORINTHIANS 3. 10–20

How We Build

We shall not understand these particular words, unless we appreciate their historical context. Corinth had been destroyed in 146 B.C. and partially rebuilt one hundred years later by Julius Caesar. The result was that alongside splendid buildings, enriched with pillars of marble and porphyry, and adorned with silver and gold, were to be seen the pitiable hovels of the poor. Corinth was spoiled by careless building. Paul knew that a sound foundation had been laid in the Church since he had laid it carefully himself. We are God's temple (v. 16). We exist for His glory. We need to take heed to our building.

1. WE MUST TAKE HEED TO THE FOUNDATION vv. 10-11

There must obviously be a firm foundation. The missionary knows this only too well when he introduces the Christian faith into some new area. All that follows will depend upon first efforts.

(a) There can only be *One Firm Foundation*, that is, Christ (v. 11). It is tragically easy to attempt church building on other grounds. It is possible to attempt church building on the foundation of social service, or moral force, rather than that of redemptive power.

(b) There can only be *One Enduring Foundation*. Other foundations will crumble and the church will fall. There may be a time when social service is not so vital, or moral force apparently unnecessary, but Christ and His redemptive message is always needed. On the confession of Christ the church is built. It is against this confession the gates of hell can never prevail.

(c) There can be only *One Complete Foundation*. Christianity is not a mixture of revelation and philosophy, or human endeavour and Divine righteousness. It is a work which is completely of God. We must see to it that we are building upon Christ and Christ alone.

2. WE MUST TAKE HEED TO THE MATERIALS WE USE vv. 12-13

As ministers we need to ask ourselves: 'What materials are we putting into our ministry?' What is the content of our preaching? Are we pandering to the popular taste? Are we failing to give the whole counsel of God? Is the ministry being built up around popularity and pulpit oratory and little else?

As Christians what materials are we putting into our lives? What is the nature of our spiritual diet? Are we attempting to satisfy our spiritual hunger with tasty spiritual titbits? Paul distinguishes

26

between the durable material such as was to be seen in the great buildings of Corinth, and the perishable commodities which were used in the construction of the mud hovels. The searching judgement of God will reveal the kind of material we are building into our lives.

3. WE MUST TAKE HEED TO THE FASHION IN WHICH WE BUILD vv. 16–17

The builder must have his architect. The emphasis in modern building is on design. How many Christians there are who have no design for living; no real purpose in life. They know nothing of the Lord's will; they are content to follow their own inclination and muddle through to glory. They may, like an ill designed house, have the right things in the wrong places. They are

'Building a house not made with hands', but are not
'Following Jesus' perfect plans'.

4. WE MUST TAKE HEED THAT WE BUILD FOR THE FUTURE vv. 14–15

Paul declares that the day of judgement will test our lives. When men built in centuries past they built for the future. Their churches and houses still stand. They have withstood the ravages of time.

I CORINTHIANS 3. 21–23

The Limitless Possessions of the Christian

Although the church at Corinth boasted of its gifts, in reality it was spiritually poor, or at least it failed to realise its wealth. It had narrowed its horizons. Such was the tragic result of its sectarian spirit. They needed to possess their possessions.

1. They needed to learn *THE VALUE OF A RIGHT PERSPECTIVE*

We limit the love of God. We talk of truth as if it could be condensed to the size of our puny minds. We do not realise that the waves which wash our feet are but an infinitesimal fraction of the mighty ocean which breaks upon every shore. The trouble is that our eyes become blinded by the mists of time and sense, our thoughts narrowed by the well worn paths of prejudice. We are content to live in the darkened corner when we could enjoy the panoramic view from the mountain top. We have such a vantage point in Christ. Schools of thought there must ever be, or truth would die. Let us recognise their value, claim the truth they teach, yet not be lost among them. Christianity is larger than life. In Corinth they were blinded by the many lights that shone; they could not see that they were but broken lights of Him, who is the source of all light, the Light of the world.

2. They needed to learn *THE IMMENSITY OF THEIR POSSESSIONS IN CHRIST*

'All things are yours' (v. 21). The Stoics said that 'All things belong to the wise'. Paul went further he specified what these things are.

(a) *The world of personalities is ours.* Paul, Apollos and Cephas belonged to all. Here was their bone of contention. One said, 'I am of Paul', another, 'I of Cephas', yet another, 'I of Apollos'. These men were not contradictory but complementary. Paul was the theologian, Apollos the preacher, Peter the organiser. All are necessary to the church.

(b) *The world of nature is ours,* with its majesty and infinite variety. The world which delights the eye and gladdens the heart. The song of the bird and the roar of the mountain torrent. 'All things are yours.'

(c) *The world with its range of experience,* between the cradle and the grave, life and death is ours. Paul was able as a Christian to write to the Philippians 'For me to live is Christ and to die is gain' (Phil. 1.21).

28

(*d*) *The world of the present and the world to come is ours*. God has put eternity into our hearts. When we stand in this world we can see vistas of the world to come through the eye of faith.

3. They needed to learn *WHOSE THEY WERE AND WHOM THEY SERVE*

'Ye are Christ's, and Christ is God's' (v. 23). Our possessions are ours, in Christ, and through Christ. These are God's gifts to men, but they are of grace and grace is ours through Christ. Christ is the link that binds us to God. A peasant girl married to a prince enjoys the wealth of his kingdom, but only because of her relationship to the prince. It is His love which brings us into the glory and wealth of the Father's home.

I CORINTHIANS 4. 1–21

Personal Relationships

There is nothing more likely to destroy the fellowship of God's people than harsh criticism and unkind judgements. This had been proved conclusively in the church at Corinth. Incipient sectarianism had led to such. Our Lord had warned His disciples, 'Judge not, that ye be not judged' (Matt. 7.1). This is a word much needed, yet it is a word little heeded. This chapter falls into three divisions.

1. We are warned against *JUDGING GOD'S SERVANTS* vv. 1–7

Paul had no quarrel with Apollos, neither did Apollos with Paul, and certainly Peter was on good terms with both. The wrangling was caused by their partisans. It was a sad case of 'minister worship'. Unfortunately evangelicalism has far too often been spoiled by the cult of the preaching personality. Men and women have flocked to the man with outstanding oratorical gifts, rather than to the house of God to worship. Let us appreciate the nature of the minister's task.

(a) Paul refers to the minister as *A Steward* (v. 1). Dr. G. Campbell Morgan points out that literally the word means 'housekeeper'. A steward was a responsible slave in a Roman household. He was responsible for its management. We are responsible for the 'mysteries' of God, that is, the wonderful plan of redemption which once was unknown, but now has been revealed to us.

(b) Paul points out that *Faithfulness* is the supreme quality required in a steward. God does not ask that we be successful, but that we be faithful (v. 2).

(c) Paul adds that the *Judgement of God's Servants* is not our task, nor is it something that can be carried out now. Our judgements are liable to be prejudiced. A historian refuses to judge events too near to his own time. The judgement of God's servants must be left until the judgement seat of Christ (v. 5).

2. The apostle suggests that we should *JUDGE OURSELVES* vv. 8–17

When we are busy judging others we have no time to judge ourselves. Paul does two things in this section.

(a) *He exposes their self esteem.* They were engaged in the setting off of one servant of God against another, emphasising their differences. Truly there were differences, Apollos was an orator, Paul was a theologian, Peter was an evangelist, but who had made them such? Was it not the God who imparts to us several gifts? In verse 8 he points out that they claimed to be living the regnant life. He wished that they were, but alas the very opposite was the case. They claimed to be sovereigns, but they were living like slaves.

(b) *He points to the selfless example of the apostles* (vv. 10–17). He contrasts their empty boasts with the reality of their position, weak, despised, hungry, thirsty, buffeted, etc. He employs the picture of a gladiator in the arena, a pitiable spectacle for the world to gaze upon.

3. We are introduced to the subject of *GOD'S WILL*, and challenged as to our *REACTION TO IT* vv. 18–21

There were those in Corinth who said Paul would never visit the city again. Paul made it clear that he certainly would visit the city, not to listen to their wrangling but to demonstrate the power of the Kingdom. For these wrangling Corinthians, Christianity was merely a matter of words, for Paul it was a dynamic (v. 20). Notice the three 'wills' in this closing section of the chapter, 'I will' (v. 19), 'if the Lord will' (v. 19), 'what will ye?' (v. 21). Our wills function, but they are subservient to the Lord's will. It is up to us whether God acts in judgement or in mercy. Our response to His will decides.

1 CORINTHIANS 5. 1–13

Purging out the Old Leaven

We live in an age of indiscipline. There is neither the discipline in the home nor in the school that once there was, and now we are beginning to reap the bitter harvest in society. It is not therefore surprising that there is little discipline exercised within the church. Evil is often tolerated as a private affair; scriptural injunctions are not obeyed; scriptural principles are not applied. How can the church be revived and cleansed? The answer is suggested to us in this chapter.

1. There must be *A RECOGNITION OF EVIL*

We must be prepared to recognise evil wherever it exists. It must be brought out into the light and dealt with. A man who is suffering from a disease which could prove fatal, but who endures his pain and discomfort rather than go to a doctor and discover the nature of his malady, is most foolish. Notice how Paul dealt with the problem.

(*a*) *He exposes the sin* (v. 1). Some commentators believe that Paul is here referring to incest. If it was not incest it was not far removed therefrom. A member of the church had committed adultery with either his stepmother, or a former mistress of his father. In pagan society immorality was common; indeed, many of the pagan cults condoned immorality and even encouraged it. If we are to know the Lord's cleansing in our lives, then we must confess our sin specifically to God. A 'general confession' is not enough.

(b) *He condemns the acquiescence of the church* (v. 2). The church was as guilty as the people concerned in the act of sin. Indeed there were some in the church who gloried in the tolerance shown to the sinners within its midst. Is it not so today in our world, if not in the church? Men pride themselves on their broadmindedness, and sin remains unjudged.

(c) *He makes his own position clear* (v. 3). Paul never pandered to popular opinion. Where discipline had to be administered he imposed such, and left the issue with God.

2. There must be a *DENUNCIATION OF EVIL*

It is relatively easy to recognise evil, to say that something or other is sinful, but it is not so easy to execute judgement. This is where the ecclesiastical machine breaks down. How can we judge our fellows when we are so prone to sin ourselves? Paul gives some practical advice in this chapter.

(a) *He names the authority by which we must judge and exercise discipline* (v. 4). 'The name of our Lord Jesus Christ . . . with the power of our Lord Jesus Christ.' Church discipline is not the act of one sinful man judging another, it is the exercise of Christ's power and authority. This of course is all the more reason why we should not abuse this authority, but always exercise it with due care and restraint.

(b) *He points out that it is a church matter.* It is the act of the community towards the individual. Indeed it is the self preserving action of the community. Verse 4 makes this clear, judgement is to be carried out when the church is 'gathered together'.

(c) *He makes it clear that the purpose of judgement is the eventual blessing of the sinner* (v. 5). The phrase 'to deliver such a one unto

32

Satan' is difficult to explain. It seems to have been a common phrase in apostolic times (cp. 2 Cor. 13.10). Simply it may be taken to mean the sinner must be allowed to suffer the physical and social penalty of his or her sin, so that he or she may realise that sin brings suffering to the sinner. Obviously it does not mean the believer is given back to Satan, from whose power he has been redeemed.

(*d*) *He points to a principle which must be applied* (v. 6). No doubt he was thinking of the Jewish custom at Passover time, of searching the house for leaven, a symbol of evil, and then destroying it. It was sin which took Christ to the Cross, how then can we condone sin in our own lives, or that of the church (v. 7)?

3. There must be *A SEPARATION FROM EVIL*

Paul teaches plainly that those who have been found guilty of sin should not be allowed the fellowship of the church during a time of discipline. This may seem terribly un-Christian, and yet missionaries have found it to be essential to the welfare of the church. Other societies exercise such discipline upon their members. Is it then wrong for the church to exercise discipline to preserve the health and holiness of its life?

1 CORINTHIANS 6. 1–20

Truths which every Christian should know

'Know ye not?' (vv. 2, 3, 9, 15, 19) was a favourite expression of Paul's. It occurs no less than ten times in the scope of the two Corinthian epistles. Dr. G. Campbell Morgan writes, 'Here we see the Apostle dealing with local matters in the light of eternal and universal truths. It is with these principles we are particularly concerned'. In Corinth they appear to have been ignorant of these principles. (Are we?) Hence the repetition of this phrase, 'Know ye not'.

1. Are we ignorant of the *JUDGEMENT WHICH THE SAINTS MUST EXERCISE?* v. 2

Not only were there dissensions at Corinth over church leaders, worse still, there were legal disputes and church members were being hauled before local pagan magistrates. Notice how Paul deals with the situation.

(*a*) *He points out the indignity to which the church is subjected* (v. 1). Pagan magistrates are referred to as 'the unrighteous', and often they most certainly were. How can the church witness effectively if its internal dissensions are made a public spectacle? The church must preserve its public image.

(*b*) *He points to the responsibility of the saints in judging the world.* This was prevalent idea in the intertestamental period. It is referred to in Wisdom of Solomon (3.8) and Daniel (7.22). If this is so, then surely Christian believers are capable of settling their differences without going to law. The world is ever eager to pass its judgement upon the church, but the church must always be the conscience of the community. It is the saints who judge the world.

(*c*) *He suggests a remedy for this regrettable state of affairs.* If there is a difference of opinion then let the matter be settled by some wise and respected member. On no account should a Christian take a fellow member to court; rather he should be prepared to suffer wrong than bring the testimony to Christ into disrepute.

2. Are we ignorant of the *CHARACTER OF THE KINGDOM?* v. 9

Let us remember there are two rival kingdoms, those of God and Satan. There is a clear line of demarcation between them. We belong to either one or the other. That line was not clearly discernible in Corinth. It should have been. The sins of the city were to be found within the life of the church. It is always a serious state of affairs when there is nothing distinctive about a local church; that is, when its membership is no different in conduct from those who make no claim to be Christian. It is therefore right that we should be clear as to the demands of the kingdom of God.

(*a*) *Those who cannot enter the Kingdom of God* (vv. 9, 10). We need to notice that this list is wide in its scope. We may not have expected to find a mention of effeminate, covetous, or extortioners. Let us beware lest we fall into any of these categories.

(*b*) *How we can be made fit to enter the Kingdom of God* (v. 11). To be fit morally we must be washed; to be fit positionally we must be set apart or sanctified; and to be fit judicially we must be justified.

(*c*) *The principle of liberty for the Christian* (v. 12). 'All things are lawful . . . but I will not be brought under the power of any.' It is a principle which must be constantly applied. We must ever guard our liberty as sons of God. No man must tell us what not to do, but at the same time in our freedom we must never allow anything to bring us into its bondage. We must ever stand fast in the liberty which is ours in Christ. In God's kingdom there is liberty, but never licence.

3. Are we ignorant of the *SANCTITY OF THE BODY*?

In the grossly immoral city of Corinth, controversy within the church centred on the body. The body is the agent of the human spirit for either good or evil. Paul points to three important facts.

(*a*) *The body is for the Lord.* This is its purpose. It has been created by God for God. God sustains what He has created, 'the Lord is for the body' (v. 13). Paul called upon the Roman believers to 'present their bodies a living sacrifice' (Rom. 12.1).

(*b*) *The body will be raised at the resurrection.* This is the prospect for the body (v. 14). We must treat our bodies in the light of this resurrection truth.

(*c*) *The body is a member of Christ* (v. 15). He must possess the body. God is interested in the 'whole man', not merely in souls divorced from bodies. We must be healthy as well as holy agents for Him.

Christian Marriage

This chapter introduces us to the twin problems of separation and divorce, problems which not only vexed the Corinthian church, but also the contemporary church. Divorce has now been brought within easy reach of the masses. Within this century there has come the emancipation of women; two world wars with a resultant lowering of moral standards and of late open rebellion against them. Paul has some useful advice to give.

1. He makes clear that *THE PROBLEM MUST BE APPRECIATED*

There are those who maintain that such subjects form no part of pulpit preaching. The fact that they are to be found within the Bible is authority enough for our dealing with them. Christianity is concerned with all of life's relationships. The Bible would not be a Divine Directory of Life if these were not included. Notice what Paul writes.

(*a*) He maintains *Its Negation in Certain Circumstances*. Verse 1 means that in some circumstances it is good that a man does not marry. This is proved in verses 5, 32–36 and 40. In verse 26 he mentions 'the present distress'. Paul well knew the possibility of martyrdom. Those who were likely to die as martyrs were well advised against marriage. Paul is not advising celibacy for all; he is merely pointing to its wisdom in certain circumstances.

(*b*) He maintains *The Necessity of it in Other Circumstances* (v. 2). The Bible does not teach that sex is immoral, it is the abuse of sex which is immoral. The sex instinct is God given. Marriage sanctifies it, setting it apart for the procreation of children and the establishment of happy family life. God knows the force of human instincts and has provided channels in which they may express themselves and find their satisfaction.

(*c*) He points to *Its Nature in All Circumstances* (v. 2). The principle Paul lays down is 'One man one wife'. Marriage must be monogamous. Marriage must be based not only on love but also fidelity. This is what he declares here, 'Let every man have his own wife, and let every woman have her own husband'.

2. He makes clear too that *THE PRINCIPLES FOR SUCCESSFUL MARRIAGE MUST BE APPLIED*

So many marriages fail because there is no real understanding of what is involved in marriage. Paul points to two things.

(*a*) *The recognition of mutual rights.* 'Let the husband render unto the wife due benevolence' (v. 3). The word 'benevolence' is an unfortunate translation. It is not to be found in some MSS. It is probably the fumbling word of some copyist. It should be translated, 'Let every man render unto the wife her due, and likewise also, the wife unto the husband'. There is mutual responsibility in marriage.

(*b*) *Respect for the marriage relationship* (v. 4). Marriage makes the man and wife one, not only in the eyes of the law but also in the sight of the Lord. Marriage is first and foremost a spiritual union, hence the warning against the unequal yoke.

3. The apostle points to the *PROCEDURE TO BE ADOPTED IN SOME CASES*

Good though it is to appreciate the problem; salutary though it is to know the principles that must be applied if marriage is to be successful, Paul does not stop there. He lays down procedure that should be adopted in certain cases.

(*a*) *In the case of the unmarried and the widow* (vv. 8, 9). Many women were widowed as a result of the martyrdom of their husbands. Obviously they were the responsibility of the church. Paul advises that these widows should not rush into a hasty remarriage, nor should they allow their widowhood to be an occasion for immoral living.

(*b*) *In the case of those who are equally yoked together in marriage.* Paul advises against separation and divorce. When our Lord was questioned about the permissibility of divorce, He went back beyond the law of Moses to the institution of marriage in Eden. He pointed out that marriage was meant to be indissoluble, but Moses permitted divorce because of the hardness of their hearts.

(c) *In the case of those who were unequally yoked in marriage.* Here was a real problem in Corinth, and here is a very real problem today. Should the believing partner leave the home? Paul gives a definite 'No' to this question. The Jewish law advocated separation, but we are under grace not under law. The believing partner is a power for good in the home.

I CORINTHIANS 7. 18–40

Caring for the Things of the Lord

In these verses although Paul still has in mind the problem of marriage and divorce, the scope of his thinking broadens. He deals here with the application of spiritual principles, not only in domestic life, but also in life generally. He deals with relationships and responsibilities.

1. We must sanctify *OUR RELATIONS WITH THOSE IN THE FELLOWSHIP OF THE CHURCH*

We may not be able to change our social status. Although we may be able to change our nationality we cannot change our race. Race, social status, denominational affiliation are external matters, it matters not what they happen to be. The vital thing for the Christian is his fidelity in the service of the Lord.

Some Jews tried to cover the marks of their circumcision in the gymnasium, while mingling with Greeks. Other Jews demanded that Gentile Christians should subject themselves to the rite of circumcision (vv. 18–20). Many Christian slaves belonging to Christian masters expected to be freed after conversion. Paul gave them no encouragement in this, rather he demanded of them that they should be faithful in their service for the Lord.

In verse 23 we have an allusion to the freeing of a slave. A slave might buy his freedom. The money was deposited with the pagan priest. When enough money was saved by the slave, then both

38

master and slave went to the temple where sacrifice was offered. Then the money was paid by the priest to the master before witnesses and the slave was said to be free of his master, but became the property of the god. We have been freed from sin and Satan, but now we are God's.

2. We must realise *OUR RESPONSIBILITIES TO THOSE IN THE CIRCLE OF THE FAMILY*

The early church expected an immediate return of the Lord. This was quite understandable, especially in view of the persecution they had to face, which many of them thought to be the predicted final tribulation. There was a temptation to forsake domestic commitments. Some deserted their wives (v. 27), others advocated the celibacy of all. Paul points out here that there was something to be said for celibacy in view of the 'present distress' (v. 26). Men should not take on domestic responsibilities if they are unlikely to be able to shoulder them. Obviously much of what Paul writes here is not applicable to us in our day, but the principles he lays down are timeless and applicable in every age and circumstance. Never before was it so vital for us as preachers to emphasise the responsibilities involved in marriage and parenthood. Are we not as conscious of the transience of fashion (v. 31) as Paul was? Let us admit the truth of Paul's words in verses 32–34. There are those who feel that they can serve the Lord better if they remain unmarried. Those who are married must never allow their service for the Lord to be an excuse for neglecting their domestic responsibilities.

3. We must always be careful of *OUR CONDUCT AS BELIEVERS UNITED TO THE LORD*

The closing verses give guidance to parents concerning the marriage of their children, and in verse 39 the apostle emphasises the binding nature of the marriage bond. In this verse he makes it clear that if a widow remarry it must be 'in the Lord'. Indeed whatever we do, whatever relationship we enter into with others, it must be 'in the Lord'. Here is our calling (vv. 20, 24) and here we must abide.

The Weaker Brother

This chapter introduces us to the problem of meat which had been dedicated at heathen shrines. Most of the meat sold in the meat market, or the 'Shambles' as it was called, had first been dedicated at some heathen shrine or other. Should a Christian partake of that which had been so dedicated? By partaking of it was he compromising his testimony? It was a controversial issue among Christians in Paul's day. Some maintained that by eating such meat they certainly did compromise their testimony, while others, denying the existence of heathen gods, affirmed that there was no danger of compromise at all. The issue may seem trivial to us, but it was a burning question to these early Christians. Behind the issue there is a principle, namely, the use which we make of our freedom as Christians.

1. There is *THE PROBLEM WHICH MUST BE APPRECIATED*

There was much to be said in favour of both arguments. Paul recognised this. At the centre of the controversy was the knowledge that the meat had been offered at a pagan shrine. The knowledge to some was hurtful to the conscience. To others it did not matter in the least. Indeed they boasted that they denied the existence of pagan gods, and accused their opponents of recognising heathen deities. Consequently in this chapter Paul deals with this question of 'knowledge'. Mark how often the words 'know' or 'knowledge' occurs.

(*a*) *He points to the pride that is often associated with knowledge* (v. 1). Knowledge may make us boastful. Pride is always dangerous.

(*b*) *He points to the limitation of knowledge* (v. 2). However much we may boast of knowing, there is always so much we are ignorant of. Further, all men do not share the same knowledge, some are more informed than others (v. 7).

(*c*) *He points to the responsibility which knowledge carries with it* (v. 11). If we have a superior knowledge it is not that we might boast, it is rather that we might be of service to others.

2. There is *A PRINCIPLE WHICH MUST BE APPLIED*

Knowledge must always be controlled by love. This love must be Divine love. Our love for God is our response to His love for us. Paul takes this issue on to a higher level. The rival factions in Corinth were considering only themselves, and their own satisfaction. Paul shows that this is an issue which concerns the Lord (v. 11).

(*a*) *It is in God that love and knowledge meet.* It is in God that they work together for man's good. They must work together in us for the good of others. The weaker brother must always be considered.

(*b*) *Knowledge merely puffs up.* It does not bring strength with it. Love with knowledge 'builds up' (v. 1). Our duty is not to fill ourselves with pride through knowledge, but edify our brethren in the Lord.

3. There is *A PATH WE MUST TREAD*

It is the path of self denial for the good of others. No man can live to himself. We are tied up together in the bundle of life. We must not be unmindful of the weaker brother.

1 CORINTHIANS 9. 1–18

In Defence of Apostleship

There were those in Corinth who denied that Paul was an apostle. They maintained that he was not one of the original disciple band, and had not been a witness of the resurrection—the essential ingredient of apostleship. An apostle is a 'sent one', so there is a sense therefore in which we are all apostles, in that we are all called and sent by God as His ambassadors in the world. Frequently we have to defend our apostleship as Paul did here. We do well to mark Paul's method.

1. He refers to *HIS PERSONAL EXPERIENCE OF CHRIST*

This is where we must all begin; with what we know of Christ from personal experience. We cannot proclaim another's Christ as the sons of Sceva sought to do (Acts 19.15). It is not enough for us to believe that Christ is Saviour of the world. First and foremost, He must be ours. What is involved in this personal experience?

(*a*) *A vision of Christ* (v. 1). The original disciple band had personally seen the risen Christ. They had met him in the upper room and at the lakeside. They had gazed on the marks of His suffering. It is true we cannot see Him with our physical eyes, but we can discern Him with the eye of faith.

(*b*) *Fruit of Christ's power in the lives of others* (v. 2). There is no better way of confirming our faith than that of bringing others to Christ and witnessing the work of the Spirit in their lives. We are always God's apostle to those whom we are instrumental in bringing to Christ.

(*c*) *The freedom which we enjoy* (vv. 1, 3). He was free to respond to God's call and serve the Divine cause. We can go for Christ, because we have been freed from the shackles of sin by Him.

2. He refers to *THE AUTHORITY HE RECEIVED FROM GOD*

It was necessary for Paul to stress his authority and remind his critics of his 'rights'.

(*a*) *His personal freedom* (v. 1). This carried with it normal social rights, such as that to 'eat and drink' and marry if he so desired. Paul may not have been married, but he maintains his right to marry. He was in bondage to no man, but was ever subject to the authority of God. Our freedom comes from our subjection to Christ.

(*b*) *His right of maintenance as a servant of God* (vv. 7 ff.). Just as the soldier has a right to be paid for his services; the vinedresser lives of the fruit of his vine, and the shepherd of the flock he tends, so Paul could expect support from those among whom he ministered. This was both scriptural and historical. The law of

Moses allowed the ox to feed from the grain it trod, also the priests and Levites in Israel were supported by the tithes of the people.

(c) *His right to expect a spiritual harvest as a reward for his work* (v. 11). Alas, in Corinth, though Paul had sowed spiritual seed, he was reaping a carnal harvest because of the carnality of the Christians in the city.

3. He refers to the *NECESSITY LAID UPON HIM BY THE GOSPEL* v. 16

In spite of all that Paul was entitled to, he did not demand anything as of right. He worked with his own hands to support himself. He was conscious that when he had done all that was required of him he had no reason to boast of his labours. He had a debt to God that the labours of his hands could never repay. He would ever be God's debtor. It was necessary for him as the bond slave of Christ to preach the gospel. The proclamation of the gospel is an obligation laid upon us all.

I CORINTHIANS 9. 19–27

For the Gospel's Sake

No matter where he might be, Paul was ever a herald of the gospel. In the work of the gospel he was no man's debtor, though he had every right to be. This he makes abundantly clear in the former part of this chapter. He has made himself free from all men that he might be the servant of all (v. 19). These verses are primarily meant for the Christian worker, particularly those who are engaged in full time Christian service, but they have a message for all believers.

1. Here we learn *PAUL'S PRINCIPLE* vv. 19–22a

Though the apostle had been born a Jew and raised as a Pharisee, God had called him to be the apostle to the Gentile. He gloried in the liberty he enjoyed in Christ. He delighted in the fact that he had not been brought to the Lord through any human agency, but by direct revelation on the Damascus road. There, he had heard the commission of the risen Christ (Gal. 1.11, 12). No man could claim that Paul was the product of his particular brand of preaching, not even Ananias, who kindly received him after his conversion.

Paul did not have to follow any particular path so as to please some other Christian. He was directly responsible to the Lord alone, and because of this, he felt free to adapt himself to the needs of those to whom he ministered. He could be 'all things to all men' in the Pauline sense of the phrase. By this, he meant that he was able because of the variety of his experience to gear his message to the experience of his hearers. We must notice how Paul's epistles are full of allusions to the background of his readers, e.g. Philippi was a Roman colony, consequently he reminds the church there, it is a 'colony of heaven' (such is the meaning of Phil. 3.20, where 'conversation' means 'citizenship'); Rome boasted of its power, consequently Paul writes of the power of the gospel in his Roman epistle (Rom. 1.16). George Fox once said, 'I have prayed to be baptised into a sense of all conditions that I might be able to know the needs and feel the sorrows of all'. This was Paul's principle too. He began his work not from some theological platform, but with the needs of men to whom he ministered. Like his Master he met men at the point of their need, and so must we.

2. Here too we learn *PAUL'S PURPOSE* v. 22b

It was ever to win men for Christ. This is something that we must constantly bear in mind. We must ever examine our motives. It is tragically possible to be engaged in Christian service for the popularity it brings, or for the sense of satisfaction it brings to us, or even for the financial reward which results. We cannot gain all, though we minister to all, but we can gain 'some'. We must ever remember that the value of one soul is worth all and indeed more than all the energy we expend in the service of the Master. We must make Paul's purpose ours too.

3. Here further we learn of *PAUL'S PROSPECT* v. 24

That prospect was a prize (v. 24). If we would receive the 'Well done', then we must subject ourselves to the discipline of service, just as the athlete subjects himself to the discipline of training that he might be successful in the games. Paul told the Thessalonian believers that they were his 'crown of rejoicing' (1 Thess. 2.19).

4. Here also we learn of *PAUL'S PERIL* v. 27

The Greek word means 'disapproved'. It is used by the refiner of metals. It is a challenging thought that we can serve, yet because of indiscipline we may find ourselves lacking the Lord's approval.

I CORINTHIANS 10. 1–14

Learning from the Past

It is often said, and quite rightly,

'The New is in the Old contained,
The Old is by the New explained.'

We have proof of it here in these verses. Paul makes it clear that the record of Israel's history is a parable of the believer's experience. We can learn from the fortunes and the failures of the past.

1. We can learn from *ISRAEL'S EXPERIENCE OF GOD*

Paul begins with that favourite sentence of his, 'I would not that ye should be ignorant', and then goes on to refer to Israel's history; the experience of God's people in the days of the wilderness wanderings. We do well to note the nature of this experience.

(*a*) It was an experience of *God's Guiding and Protective Power* (v. 1). They were 'under the cloud'. When Israel passed through the Red Sea the cloud stood between them and the advancing Egyptian host. It acted as a light to Israel and darkness to the

45

enemy. As they trekked through the wilderness it went before them. It was vital that they moved with the cloud. It is essential that we too keep in step with God.

(b) It was an experience of *Their Subjection to God's Appointed Leader* (v. 2). This is what Paul means by being 'baptised unto Moses'. Israel were identified with Moses, they obeyed Moses' commands. To the Egyptians they were Moses' men. It is so with us. When we become Christians we are identified with Christ, we become Christ's men.

(c) It was an experience of *God's Provision* (vv. 3, 4). God wonderfully supplied the needs of His pilgrim people. There was manna to eat and water from the rock to drink. Verse 4 is difficult to interpret. Obviously it cannot be interpreted literally. It seems best to hold that what God was to Israel in the wilderness, Christ is to us in the wilderness of this world. This is surely the principal point of this passage.

2. We can learn from *ISRAEL'S UNFAITHFULNESS TO GOD*

We might think that a people so privileged, and so singularly blessed, would have been wholly devoted to God. But alas, not all were. Mark the contrast between 'all' and 'some' in these verses. Notice, too, that tragic little word of three letters at the beginning of verse 5, 'but'. 'But with many of them God was not well pleased.' These perished in the wilderness. This was never God's intention. His purpose was that they should possess Canaan. 'He brought them out that He might bring them in'. Such is God's purpose for us. He has delivered from the penalty of sin, that we might enter into the fulness of His blessing. How were Israel unfaithful?

(a) *They were idolaters* (v. 7). When Moses went up the mountain to receive the tablets of stone, Israel turned to idolatry. Are we not often guilty of the same sin? Whatever comes between us and God is an idol. How often we allow even the legitimate things of life to rob us of communion with God!

(b) *They engaged in lustful pursuits* (v. 8). The flesh is ever with us demanding gratification. We are very prone to give way to it.

If we examine our lives in the light of the Spirit, somewhere or other, we are likely to find a proneness to give way to some lust of the flesh.

(c) *They grumbled even when they were blessed with God's goodness* (vv. 9, 10). They tried God's patience and murmured against His goodness. Are we guilty of this too?

3. We can gain STRENGTH AND COMFORT FROM PAUL'S WORDS

We need not despair. God knows the weakness of this mortal frame (v. 13). We need not think that our temptations are peculiar to us. If God permits us to be tested, He does not allow us to be placed in such a position that we must succumb. However, we must never place ourselves in such a position that we find ourselves courting temptation. We must 'flee idolatry' (v. 14).

I CORINTHIANS 10. 15–33

The Lord's Table

The key verse to this section of the chapter is verse 31. In the closing injunction we have the Christian's motive, namely, 'the glory of God'. It was inevitable that the advent of Christianity into the lives of these Corinthians should present many problems. We must remember that the whole fabric of Corinthian life was impregnated with paganism. Even the meat they ate had first been dedicated at a heathen shrine. Questions of conduct were constantly being raised by Christians in Corinth. The problems which faced these Corinthian Christians may not be the problems which face us, but the principles behind them are the same. Whatever we do, however we act, we must 'do all to the glory of God'.

1. We must remember that *AT THE LORD'S TABLE WE SHARE THE FELLOWSHIP OF THE MASTER* vv. 16–17

The cup is the communion of His blood, the bread of His body. The Jewish Passover was a family occasion, the head of the house officiated. In the upper room Christ took the cup as head of the family. Not only do we enjoy union with Christ, in that we are 'in Him', we have communion 'with Him'. The Lord's Table should be the one place where we are most conscious of our fellowship with Him and with all who love His name. Alas, it has become in the hands of men, the barrier to fellowship.

2. We must remember too that *THE LORD'S TABLE INVOLVES OUR SEPARATION FROM THE WORLD TO CHRIST* v. 21

Separation is a doctrine little taught in our churches, largely, no doubt, because it is little understood. Our attendance at the Lord's Supper demands our dedication to the Lord. Paul points out that meat offered at heathen shrines was still meat, and the idols themselves were nothing more than 'sticks and stones'. The evil lay in the thought behind the idols, the demonic power which held sway over men's minds. Participation in pagan rites involved acknowledgement of demonic powers. We cannot run with the hare and hunt with the hounds in the Christian life. The Lord's supper is a sacrament which binds us to Christ.

3. Further we must remember that *THE LORD'S TABLE DEMANDS THAT WE BE DISCREET* vv. 23–29

We must not become stumbling blocks to others (v. 23). If there is no danger of causing another to stumble, then we are free to act within the limits of our own conscience, but should there be a danger to others, then we must respect their consciences. The word translated 'wealth' (v. 24) should be rendered 'good' or 'welfare'. The principle is that we should not live merely to please ourselves, but to the 'glory of God' which ensures the welfare of others.

48

4. Finally, we must remember that *THE LORD'S TABLE INVOLVES US IN SEEKING THE GLORY OF GOD*

This is the message of the 'key verse' (v. 31). The Christian life is essentially a life with a purpose, and that purpose must always be the glory of God.

1 CORINTHIANS 11. 1–16

Courtesy in the Church

It can be said that this is 'the epistle of knowledge'. In chapter 6 no less than six times Paul uses the phrase, 'Know ye not?' Here, too, the apostle emphasises the need for knowledge. In chapter 8, however, he points to the danger of knowledge, 'knowledge puffeth up', while in chapter 13 he refers to the inadequacy of knowledge, 'though I . . . understand all mysteries, and all knowledge, and have not love, I am nothing'. There is a need for knowledge. God does not set any premium on ignorance. Here he refers to the etiquette that as Christians and church members we should know.

1. We should know that there is *AN ORDER OF CREATION*

Paul is concerned with courtesy within the church, the way in which men and women should conduct themselves in worship. Many of the womenfolk in Corinth were so exulting in their new found freedom as Christians that they threw decorum to the winds, attending worship unveiled. Paul points out that the woman should cover her head.

(*a*) Because it is a *Condition of Creation* (v. 3). There is a priority which must be observed. Man is the head of the woman, as Christ is head of the man, and God is the head of Christ. In these days of equal pay and opportunity many find this difficult to accept, yet its truth remains.

(*b*) Because of the *Honour of the Head*. The man who worships with a covered head dishonours himself, so does the woman who worships with an uncovered head. The woman was meant to take her place at the side of the man as his help meet. Christ is the glory of man, and man the glory of woman. The veiled head is the sign of subjection.

(*c*) Because it is a *Matter of Common Sense* (v. 13). Certainly it was never meant to be a cause for contention.

2. We should know that there is *A UNITY IN THE LORD* vv. 11–12

A great deal of friction can be aroused in discussing the relation between the sexes. It is good for us as Christians to turn to God's Word and rediscover God's pattern for marriage. God brought man and woman together. The sexes are different and meant to be so. There should be no contradiction, rather they should be complementary one to the other.

The really important phrase here is 'in the Lord'. Many are married in our churches, but only those who are 'in the Lord' are so married. 'All things are of God' (v. 12). Christian marriage is the marriage that recognises the Lord's leading and seeks God's blessing.

It is in the Lord that 'we live and move and have our being'. As Christians we cannot think of entering any union which does not come within the circle of our Christian life. There would be less unhappy marriages if this were remembered by Christians.

3. We should know that there is *A NEED FOR COMELY APPEARANCE* vv. 15–16

In our own day women seek to look like men and men like women. There is really nothing more distasteful than an effeminate man and a masculine looking woman. We must remember that God is concerned about our outward appearance just as he is about our inward condition. We do not bring honour to God's name if we neglect our personal appearance.

Behaviour at the Table

Not only was there dissension in the Corinthian church, there were disorders too. Their conduct at the Lord's Table greatly distressed the apostle. There are three points we may consider in this passage.

1. *THE REBUKE PAUL DELIVERED*

The disorders had arisen because of the connection of the Lord's Supper with the *Agape*, or common meal that was held in the early church. In the Jerusalem church Christians met daily in their homes to remember the Lord (Acts 2.46). Jude in his short epistle refers to these feasts (v. 12), and the disorders often associated with them. These feasts were intended to stimulate fellowship among the believers. At Corinth they had the opposite effect. There was little difference between their love feasts and the pagan feasts of the city. The love feasts became occasions of division, gluttony and intemperance.

When they came to the Lord's Table they were in the right place, but they were there for the wrong purpose. Motive is important. It is good not to absent ourselves from the Table, but when we come we must do so, not in slavish obedience to a command, but in adoration and a spirit of dedication.

2. *THE REVELATION PAUL MADE*

It was vitally necessary that the Corinthian believers should be reminded of the original nature of the Lord's Supper. How easy it is to forget original intentions. Referring to the abuse of the Supper in his day Calvin said, 'It is portentous that Satan should have accomplished so much in so little time.' The rite of Holy Communion rests upon the Divine revelation of a historic fact (v. 23). This revelation has a fourfold spiritual significance.

(a) It speaks to us of *our Lord's Incarnation*. 'He took bread . . . and said . . . "This is my body" ' (v. 24). It reminds us that 'The

Word became flesh'. It is significant that when the Saviour came, He came not as an angel but as a man.

(b) It speaks to us of *our Lord's Redemption*. 'This is my body, which is broken for you' (v. 24). The insertion of the word 'broken' in our A.V. is questionable. It is ommitted in the R.V. The thought is not the breaking of the body, but the self sacrifice of Christ on our behalf. It is through the giving of Himself, that our redemption has been achieved.

(c) It speaks to us of *The Gospel Invitation*. 'Ye do show the Lord's death till He come' (v. 26). The Lord's death for our sin is the very heart of the gospel. When we proclaim the cross we preach the gospel. When we partake of the Lord's supper we are preaching the gospel. The hymn writer was right when he wrote, 'No gospel like this feast'.

(d) It speaks to us of *the Lord's Return*. 'Till He come' (v. 26). We must not miss these three words. Each time we remember the Lord's death in obedience to His command we not only look back to the cross we look forward to Christ's return. The Lord's Supper ever reminds us of the fact that Christ is coming back again.

3. *THE REMINDER PAUL GAVE*

In the closing verses of this chapter the apostle reminds the Corinthian believers that the Lord's Supper must never be taken lightly or thoughtlessly. It is a solemn act of remembrance. This act of remembrance calls for two things.

(a) *Self examination* (v. 28). We have been eager in our churches to 'fence' the Lord's Table, and with much justification, but first and foremost the onus of responsibility is upon the communicant himself. No one knows his heart as he does himself. If we judge ourselves now then there will be less judgement for us at the judgement seat of Christ (v. 31). The purpose of Divine judgement of the believer is his blessing (v. 32). If we allow the Lord to search our hearts through the Holy Spirit then we shall not face God's judgement which inevitably awaits an evil world.

(b) *Thoughtfulness for others* (v. 33). Although we must examine ourselves we must remember that we come together communally, and the observance of the Lord's Supper is a communal act. This is why Paul calls upon the Corinthian believers to 'tarry one for another'. We must remember that in Corinth the actual observance of the Lord's Supper was preceded by the *agape* or love feast. It seems that the *agape* had become an occasion for licence, so that the Corinthian Christians did not observe the Supper solemnly. It was a case of 'every man for himself'.

I CORINTHIANS 12. 1–11

One Body, but Many Members

This chapter marks a turning point in the epistle. As Dr. G. Campbell Morgan has commented, 'This first part of Paul's letter was wholly corrective. From this point to the end it is wholly constructive.' This chapter is important too, because it introduces the theme of the church as the 'body of Christ'. Paul was eager to emphasise the unity of the body yet at the same time the diversity of its gift. We have seen that the believers at Corinth had lost sight of the former, while they boasted of the latter. The key verse may be taken as verse 12, since it emphasises both unity and diversity of gift. The word 'body' reminds us that the church is a living organism. There are four features of the organism we must not miss.

1. *THE RECOGNITION OF ITS MASTER* v. 3

The process of human development involves mastery of the body. It means the mastery of one's limbs, the discipline of one's organs, and the control of one's mind. Where there is no such mastery then the person concerned becomes a burden to himself and to others. If the church is to function as a disciplined organism, then it must submit to the mastery of its Head. We must never forget that the church is the integration of the individual. It is only when as individuals, that we recognise the Lordship of Christ, the church is subjected to the mastery of Christ. Paul makes it clear that such men are those who, (*a*) *Have been radically changed* (v. 2). Notice the past tense, 'Ye know that ye were Gentiles, carried away unto these dumb idols'. They were outside the commonwealth of Israel, they knew nothing of the law or covenant. They were led astray by pagan priests, they had no mind of their own. They were as lifeless spiritually as the idols they worshipped. How different now! Divine life surged through their souls. It is only as we experience this life we begin to recognise its source and submit to Christ as Lord.

(*b*) *Do so in the power of the Holy Spirit* (v. 3). It appears that there were those who from time to time spoke slightingly of Jesus, probably unconverted Jews, who joined with the Christians in Corinth. It is the work of the Holy Spirit to exalt Christ. No man will speak ill of Christ who is under the control of the Holy Spirit. Indeed everyone in the Spirit will own that Jesus is Lord. The church must recognise its Master if it is to exercise its gift and be an effective witness in the world.

2. THE DIVERSITY OF ITS MINISTRY

God's plan everywhere seems to be diversity in the midst of unity. We are inclined to think that they are mutually exclusive. God makes it plain that you can have a sense of unity yet at the same time diversity. Nothing is more monotonous than uniformity. Note the nature of this diversity.

(*a*) *It is a diversity of gift* (v. 4). It means abilities or powers. Notice carefully however that Paul is eager to point out there is a unity of Spirit though diversity of gifts. Just as members of the body have various functions to perform so do members of the church. We all have our part to play.

(*b*) *It is a diversity of administration* (v. 5). The word 'administration' means literally 'opportunities' or 'services'. Different members of the body are employed on different occasions, sometimes there are those who work together at the same time. They are employed as opportunity presents itself. Again Paul emphasises unity, this time he emphasises the Lordship of Christ. Those who administer, exercise lordship themselves, but they are all subject to the lordship of Christ.

(*c*) *It is a diversity of operation*, that is of industry. The hand does not work in the same way as the foot. You cannot expect your hand to do what is meant for the foot. The machinery is designed for the task it has to perform, yet every piece of machinery is dependent upon the same power supply. There is always unity in the midst of diversity.

3. *THE UNITY OF ITS MEMBERS*

We need to follow this thought further. Unity is possible because,

(a) *The church has one distributor of its gifts*(v. 4). The human body begins in the womb as an embryo. It is a kind of rudimentary heart which gradually develops. The human body is not a prefabricated entity, made up of several parts joined together.

(b) *The church has one director of its work* (v. 5), 'the same Lord'. The body which moves uncontrolled is suffering from convulsions. This is often what is wrong with the church. It is not subjected to its Head.

(c) *The church has one dynamic in its work* (v. 6), 'the same God which worketh all in all'. We must never forget that the church is a lifeless corpse apart from God. It must never attempt to move under its own momentum. It can only be effective as its power lines to God are kept intact.

(d) *The church has one duty* (v. 7), 'to profit withal'. It is not only designed and operated by God, it is designed for God. The church does not exist to enjoy itself but to bring glory to God and extend His Kingdom.

4. *THE NATURE OF ITS GIFTS* vv. 8–11

There is some part every Christian can play. One may be able to impart the deep things of God; this is what Paul means by 'wisdom' (v. 8). Another, by his powers of reasoning, may be able to win the thinkers of this world. Yet another, by reason of his great faith, may possess the power of healing. Others will excel in bringing about mighty changes, or miracles, while some will have the ability to speak with tongues or convey the word of God in some foreign tongue or dialect. Whatever the gift, it is of the Spirit, and for the glory of God and the proper functioning of the church.

How Unity is possible and what it Means

In the remaining verses of this chapter Paul continues his great theme of unity. It might appear that he has little to add to what he has already written in the opening verses. The careful student of scripture, however, will discern here a progress of thought. He has emphasised unity, and diversity in the midst of unity. This appears to be a paradox. How can unity and diversity be reconciled, we may well ask? The answer is to be found here in these verses.

1. *IT IS THE WORK OF THE SPIRIT* v. 13

Unity of the body is possible because of our common experience of the Spirit of God. 'By one Spirit.' We talk about 'having the same spirit', meaning that a group of men and women have the same outlook, and are engaged in the same endeavour. They are united by a common purpose. This is true of the church.

(a) *'By one Spirit are we all.'* We may stop at this point, since the rather odd sentence which results emphasises a tremendous truth. The church is characterised by diversity of administrations and operations, but it owes its existence to the Spirit of God, not a multiplicity of forces at work in the world. We exist as Christians because we have all been convicted of our sin by the Spirit of God and born again by the same Spirit. 'By one Spirit are we all.'

(b) *'By one Spirit are we all baptised . . . and have been all made to drink into one Spirit.'* The latter phrase should be translated 'drenched with the same Spirit'. Obviously the thought of baptism is repeated. Baptism implies identification. It mattered not whether they were Jews or Gentiles, by the Spirit in baptism they had become one. Baptism merely confirms and expresses their unity.

(c) *'By one Spirit are we all baptised into one body.'* A new agency was brought into existence at Pentecost, an agency which transcended race. Men are frantically trying to bring the nations of the world together, to solve political and economic problems. God did

56

it in a moment at Pentecost. He does it still, immediately a soul is regenerated by the Spirit of God. By the Spirit old barriers are broken down and new members are added to the one body.

2. *IT IS THE GOOD PLEASURE OF GOD* v. 18

Verse 18 opens with one of Paul's 'But nows'. All time for Paul was divided into past and present: the past being the time before Christ is realised through the Spirit, the present being the 'now' of spiritual experience in Christ.

(*a*) '*Hath God.*' The church is the work of God the creator. The Holy Spirit is His instrument in the new creation as in the original natural creation (Gen. 1.2). We must remember when we criticise the gifts of our brethren within the church, that it is God who is at work. He is the power within them. They may merit our criticism if they do not use God's gifts aright, but never must we speak in a derogatory manner of the gift.

(*b*) '*Set the members every one of them in the body.*' Just as there was order and design in the first creation, so in the new creation. The organs of the human body are wonderfully arranged; so are the organs of Christ's body. They are placed with great care where needed that they may function aright. We are set by God to function where He has placed us.

(*c*) '*As it hath pleased Him.*' The word 'pleased' may go a little further than the Greek original would strictly permit, yet it is a happy translation, in that it conveys the pleasure which God obtains from His new creation. When our wishes are carried out, it brings us pleasure. It gladdens God's heart to see us functioning effectively, where He has set us, no matter how humble our work and station may be (vv. 23–24).

3. *IT IS THE BODY OF CHRIST* v. 27

Of course Paul did not mean that the church in Corinth was exclusively 'the body of Christ'. As some commentators point out, a better translation would be 'a body of Christ'. The apostle means that Christ is able to function through the church in Corinth. It is so with us. We cannot claim to be the body of Christ, but we are 'a body' in the sense that Christ can function through us where He has placed us. Let us see that we do indeed function effectively for Him.

I CORINTHIANS 13. 1–13

The Primacy of Love

This is one of the most beautiful passages, not only in Scripture, but in the whole of literature. 'In this chapter we enter the purest atmosphere and breathe the most fragrant odours' (G. Campbell Morgan). What a contrast it offers to the sad story of division and disorder to be found in previous chapters! Tertullian pointed out that while it came from the pen of man it was 'uttered with all the force of the Spirit'. Here Paul writes not about brotherly or human love (*philea*), but divine love (*agape*); that is, a love which only the Spirit can impart to the human heart. We find four aspects of this love presented here.

1. *ITS EXPEDIENCY* vv. 1–3

How much love is needed in our largely loveless world! Love was needed in Corinth as much as it is today. Love is necessary,

(*a*) *for speaking* (v. 1). The world has heard much oratory. It has listened to its Pitts, Gladstones and its Greys. In our own day it listened to its Churchill. It has paid attention to the theory of Quintillian, marked the practice of Demosthenes. Corinth had heard the silver tongued Apollos, but still it needed love in speech. In the Greek the sound here echoes the sense 'a sounding brass, a tinkling cymbal'. Some of our most loveless words alas, are spoken in church meetings.

(*b*) *for understanding* (v. 2). A prophet was originally known as a 'seer'; a man of knowledge, a man who was able to see further than others. The world has never been without its seers and sages. Knowledge which lacks love is a cold repulsive gift.

58 God punished Jonah for his loveless prophesying.

(*c*) *for believing* (v. 2). It is tragically possible to be a man of faith, yet a loveless soul. Faith and love must go together as they did in the church at Thessalonica (1 Thess. 1.3). Faith is often said to be the root, and love the fruit. It is possible for a plant to be almost all root, without fruit. So many Christians are like that. *James 2:14-17*

(*d*) *for giving* (v. 3). The lavish hand is not always an indication of a loving heart. The Pharisees gave their alms to be seen of men. It is even possible to give one's life for the wrong motive. There were those in the early church who ~~courted martyrdom~~ *gave their lives as martyrs* for the honour it would bring them.

2. *ITS EXPRESSION* vv. 4–7

How does love express itself? Paul gives the answer to this question in a number of pungent phrases. We can conveniently divide them into six groups to show that love,

(*a*) *suffers and sympathises* (v. 4). Love does not retaliate. How beautifully divine love is illustrated in the life of our Lord.

(*b*) *knows contentment and calm*. 'Envieth not' (v. 4). Love does not call attention to itself and seeks its own ends. The boaster is always striving and is never content. He is so intoxicated with self love he has no love for others.

(*c*) *seemly and selfless* (v. 5). Love is courteous and polite. Some pride themselves on their frankness, but often frankness is an excuse for rudeness.

(*d*) *patient and pure*. 'Not easily provoked' (v. 5). Human love is often impure, not so that which is divine; it is patient, pure and peaceable. It does not look for the worst in others, but the best.

(*e*) *believing and bearing* (v. 7). Not mere credulity. Love lifts the heavy burden and calls it light.

(*f*) *enduring and expectant* (v. 7). The wife whose husband is reported missing refuses to give up hope, because love rules her heart. Such is divine love.

3. *ITS EXPERIENCE* vv. 8–12

This love is not an unrealisable ideal, it can be the experience of every Christian. Those who have experienced this love have discovered,

(*a*) *It is Permanent*. A. Way's translation is 'Love's flower petals never fall'. In Corinth they valued the prophetic voice, the unknown tongue and knowledge; but today the prophetic voice is largely silent, the unknown tongue is only heard in some denominations, knowledge soon vanishes. Yesterday's newspaper is used to kindle today's fire. The encyclopedia of a generation ago, then worth pounds, is almost valueless today.

(*b*) *It is Progressive* (vv. 9–11). Love teaches us and matures us.

(*c*) *It is Perfective* (v. 12). Now we can only know in part, but love makes it possible for us as last to know even as we are known.

4. *ITS EXCELLENCE* v. 13

Faith and hope are great assets, but love is far greater. No wonder that Dr. Moffatt translates the opening phrase of chapter 14, 'Make love your aim'.

I CORINTHIANS 14. 1–40

Decency and Order in Worship

Chapter 13 forms a parenthesis in this epistle. In chapter 12, we have seen that Paul has made clear that while there is one body, there are many members and many gifts. He concludes the chapter by urging the Corinthian believers to covet earnestly the best gifts. In this chapter Paul makes it plain that while there are many gifts, not all have the same value. Here he lays down guidance as to the use of the gift of tongues, a gift which in recent days has once more become the subject of controversy. Consequently this chapter has much bearing upon the use of this gift today. What has Paul to write about the gift of tongues and its use?

1. He points out that *HE PREFERS THE GIFT OF PROPHECY TO THAT OF TONGUES*

Tongues was the gift in which the Corinthian church gloried, as do some sections of the Christian church today. The apostle, however, states emphatically that the gift of prophecy or inspired preaching is preferable to tongues. The practice of tongues or *glossalia* as they are called, is a phenomenon met with only here and in the Acts; although it is doubtful whether the phenomenon of Pentecost is identical to the practice of tongues in the Corinthian church. There it was probably the power to speak in the dialect of those present, here it was the practice of making ecstatic utterances. Notice what Paul has to write on the issue.

(a) *Prophecy is for public edification, tongues merely for personal edification.* The inspired preacher edifies others, the man who speaks in tongues does not even know what he is saying himself. Certainly, the man who makes an ecstatic utterance is caught up into a sphere of intimate communion with God, but it is for his own blessing.

(b) *Prophecy is preferable, because by it others are edified, by tongues self is elevated.* Tongues can become an excuse for the display of the flesh. F. W. Robertson said, 'Where there is speaking with tongues that are inarticulate and incoherent it is a kind of insipid soliloquy'.

(c) *Prophecy is preferable to tongues since sense is preferable to sound.* Where there is an unknown tongue there must be an interpreter. It takes two to do what one can do by himself in prophecy. When we come together in church, we do so for mutual edification, not merely for personal communion, not for the selfish indulgence of our own souls, not to display our gifts; but for the mutual profit and blessing of all. 'Wherefore, brethren,' writes Paul, 'covet to prophesy' (v. 39).

2. He lays down *PRINCIPLES FOR THE PRACTICE OF TONGUES*

Paul however did not forbid the use of tongues. 'Forbid not to speak with tongues' (v. 39). Indeed, he was able to state that he spoke with tongues more than all of them (v. 18). Paul was concerned with decency and order in worship.

(*a*) *In verse 13 we have the principle itself.* It is no use being able to speak in an unknown tongue if there is no power to interpret. We may be elevated in a church service but not edified, and it is edification which must ever be the controlling principle.

(*b*) *In verse 22 we are told the purpose of tongues.* They are a sign to the unbeliever. By this, Paul means they arrest attention as at Pentecost. The believer should not need to be arrested in such a way. If his faith is only excited by the phenomenal, then he is immature and unlearned.

(*c*) *In verses 23 ff. Paul points out that even when the principle and purpose of tongues has been recognised its practice still presents a problem.* There is a danger of resulting chaos, where all insist on speaking with tongues. Two or three are sufficient, and even then an interpreter must be present. If no interpreter is present, then silence is requested.

3. Finally the apostle *LAYS DOWN RULES FOR PROPRIETY IN PUBLIC WORSHIP*

There are few passages in scripture that have been as dogmatised as this one. No passage has been so wrenched from its context. Paul regulates for the woman in worship. Some of the Corinthian women had become so excited in worship, they acted improperly. Paul called upon them to cease from their chatter and argument and to find their rightful place in worship. Christianity has no wish to silence womanhood, rather it has elevated womanhood from the slavery in which it found itself. If there is to be decency and order in worship, then all that is edifying must have its place, and all who engage in worship must find their rightful place too.

The Gospel we Preach

'Gospel' (v. 1) is a great word. It comes from an Anglo Saxon word which means 'good news'. Sometimes we refer to it as 'the evangel', which is a transliteration of the Greek word employed by Paul. The apostle uses it here with reference to the resurrection. The resurrection is the good news we proclaim. It was constantly his theme. When he came to Athens, that great intellectual centre of ancient Greece, we read that he preached unto the Athenians 'Jesus and the resurrection' (Acts 17.18). These verses are not only foundational to all that follows in the remainder of the chapter, but to the whole fabric of the Christian faith. There are four facts we need to note about the gospel.

1. *ITS DELIVERY: HOW IT COMES TO US* v. 1

As the gospel came to the Corinthians, so it still comes; from God, through men, to men. Though our gospel is of God its proclamation has been entrusted to men. It was not proclaimed through the risen Christ after His resurrection, nor by means of the angelic hosts of heaven, but through mortals like ourselves. We must not miss the personal pronouns 'I declare. . . . I preached. . . . Ye have received'. 'God has so made humanity,' Dr. Farmer has written, 'that he never enters into a personal relationship with a man apart from other human persons.' Paul preached the message God had given, and the Corinthians,

(*a*) *received it* (v. 1). Literally it means 'Ye took to yourselves'. We talk about 'taking to someone'. By this we mean more than intellectual assent; rather, constant friendship which produces loyalty to a person. The author of the Fourth Gospel bewailed the fact that Christ came unto His own 'and His own received Him not' (John 1.11). That is, they did not take Him to themselves. Receiving the gospel is taking it to ourselves.

(*b*) *enjoyed it* (v. 1). 'And wherein ye stand.' By this Paul means they were enjoying the blessings of the gospel. Our western civilisation is shot through with the gospel. So many of the blessings we enjoy and take for granted are ours because of the gospel.

(c) *were being saved by it* (v. 2). The tense here is present. Paul writes about being saved rather than saved. They were not yet finally and fully saved, since salvation is a process which begins at conversion and is not finally complete until we reach heaven.

2. *ITS DEFINITION: WHAT IT IS* vv. 3–7

There is not a simpler yet fuller definition of the gospel to be found than that in verses 3–4. Notice that the gospel is something,

(a) *grounded in history* (v. 3). The facts of Christ's life, death and resurrection are not difficult to prove. That Christ died is attested by extra-Biblical sources such as Tacitus, the Roman writer, and Josephus, the Jewish historian. For evidence of the resurrection we are dependent upon the gospel narratives and the Acts. In spite of attempts to disprove the resurrection it is one of the best attested facts of history.

(b) *formulated in creed*. We believe, not only that Christ died, but that there was a redemptive purpose in His dying. He died 'for our sins'. Others have died to set their fellows free, but no one has ever been able to die for another's sins in the sense that Christ died. This is the heart of the Christian message that Christ 'died for our sins'.

(c) *revealed in scripture*. As we read the Bible, even the Old Testament, we discover that the Cross was no afterthought in the mind of God. Christ is the Lamb, as 1 Pet. 1.20 points out, 'foreordained before the foundation of the world'.

3. *ITS DYNAMIC: WHAT IT DOES*

In verses 8–10 Paul turns from the realm of history and theology to the arena of spiritual experience: 'he was seen of me'. 'By the grace of God I am what I am.' Saul the persecutor had become Paul the Christian, who himself was persecuted. This cannot be explained merely as a re-orientation of his thinking. Its power lies in the fact of God's unmerited love in Christ; for such is grace.

4. ITS DEMANDS: WHAT IT DEMANDS OF US
v. 11

We must pass on to others the message we have received ourselves: 'Therefore,' writes Paul, '. . . so we preach'. We cannot communicate the grace that comes from God Himself, but we can tell others about it, so that faith is engendered in them. 'We preach . . . ye believed.'

I CORINTHIANS 15. 12–34

The Implication of the Resurrection

There were those at Corinth who either doubted, or denied the fact of the resurrection. Epicurean philosophers with their materialist philosophy were disinterested in an after life; while the Stoics maintained that the soul alone lived on after death, becoming again a part of God who made it. It is no wonder that in this section of the chapter the apostle deals with four evident facts.

1. THEIR DOUBTS AS TO THE REALITY OF THE RESURRECTION vv. 12–19

In these verses the apostle's thought moves in the nebulous realm of supposition.

'If there be no resurrection of the dead' (v. 13).
'If Christ be not risen' (v. 14).
'If the dead rise not' (v. 16).
'If Christ be not raised' (v. 17).
'If in this life only we have hope in Christ' (v. 19).

The final resurrection at the end of the age, rests upon Christ's resurrection. Paul points out that if Christ did not rise from the dead then,

(a) *our preaching and faith is in vain* (v. 14). There is no message to proclaim as we have seen in our last study. We cannot account for the spread of Christianity apart from the resurrection. A faith founded upon a myth could not have endured for two millenia. It is the foundation of our faith. If there is no resurrection, then the whole fabric of Christianity topples to the ground. If the cross was the end, then it would be better for us to keep silent.

(b) *the testimony of the apostle is false* (v. 15). More than five hundred witnesses were wrong. We cannot trust the pages of our New Testaments. Though our Gospel records have been subjected to the most searching examination, scholars are agreed that they are authentic records of the life and ministry of Jesus.

(c) *there is no salvation from sin* (v. 17). The cross was a terrible tragedy. Far from there being anything full and final as far as the problem of evil is concerned, nothing at all was accomplished on the cross.

(d) *death is indeed the end* (vv. 18–19). If death has claimed the noblest life ever lived, then there is certainly no hope for the rest of humanity. Those who doubted the reality of the resurrection could hardly have realised the implications of their doubts. A faith that rests upon suppositions is always insecure. The Christian faith however, rests not upon supposition, but upon the glorious affirmation that Christ is risen.

2. *HIS FAITH IN THE REALITY OF THE RESURRECTION* vv. 20–22

Verse 20 commences with one of Paul's 'buts'. 'But now is Christ risen from the dead.' As J. B. Watson once put it, 'With one stroke of the pen he turns suppositious negatives into glorious positives'. Mark what this means.

(a) *Our faith is founded upon fact*. We have seen in our previous study that it is historic fact. It however is more. It is an eternal fact. Christ lives in the power of an endless life. It is the ever present 'now'. We can shout from the roof tops 'now is Christ'.

(b) *Our faith carries with it a force* (v. 22). There is a nexus between sin and death. This surely is the point of the Genesis story. In the federal head of the race, Adam, all die, but in Christ, are all made alive. This is eternal life which begins here and now, and transcends the barrier of physical death.

(c) *Our faith contains a foretaste of the future.* Christ's resurrection is the first fruit (v. 23). It is the promise of our resurrection which will take place at the Second Advent. The order is, first Christ's resurrection, then that of His people.

3. CHRIST'S VINDICATION OF THE NECESSITY OF THE RESURRECTION

At the return of Christ His work will be vindicated. It is Christ's right to reign. He reigns in the hearts of all who enthrone Him. His kingdom must come on earth. It will come when He returns at His Second Advent. Death has been conquered, its sting has been removed, but it still exists. God will not rest until death is completely destroyed. Christ executes God's purposes and when those purposes have been achieved, then He will yield up the Kingdom to God. Christ will not do this until all that has been lost through sin has been regained.

4. OUR EXPERIENCE WHICH TESTIFIES TO THE RESURRECTION vv. 29–34

Baptism for the dead seems to have been practised in Corinth (v. 29). The reason for it has been a matter of controversy, but for our purpose of exposition, the reason is not important. The fact itself points forward to the resurrection at the Second Advent. What is the point of it, the apostle asks, if there is no resurrection of the dead? Further, why risk one's life in a time of persecution if there is no hope of a future resurrection (vv. 30–32). If there is no resurrection then there is point in the conduct of both the Epicurean and the Stoic. The challenge to the Christian is ethical. In view of the resurrection; in view of the life that now is, and the life to come; we must 'awake to righteousness and sin not' (v. 34).

The Resurrection of the Body

The possibility of life after death has never ceased to intrigue men. The Greeks believed that beyond the grave there was a shadowy underworld which they called *hades*, inhabited by the immortal spirits of those who had died. The Jews had not progressed a great deal further even in Jesus' day. Belief in the resurrection was a point at issue between the Pharisees and the Sadducees. It is quite understandable that the Corinthians should need guidance in their thinking on the subject of resurrection. We do well to note carefully, what Paul writes on the subject.

1. *DEATH IS THE PRELUDE TO RESURRECTION* v. 36

Death to the unbeliever appears to be a terrible tragedy. Indeed, it is a terrible tragedy to die without any assurance as to the future. Death to the believer however, is seen in a very different light. It is the avenue by which he enters into a new and more congenial spiritual environment. Death is a common occurrence. In Genesis 3 death is said to be the consequence of sin. In Genesis 5 we read repeatedly the phrase: 'and he died'.

Though men have become so familiar with death, they have refused to believe that death is the end. Even before Christianity brought 'life and immortality to light', there were those who believed in some form of physical resurrection. Job declared that in his flesh he would see God (19.26). Isaiah affirms, 'My dead body shall arise' (26.19). In Daniel (12.2) a twofold resurrection is foretold.

Paul uses the analogy of the sown seed. Before it can germinate the seed must be buried. Death is the prelude to resurrection.

2. *THE CHANGE RESURRECTION BRINGS ABOUT*

Many have been puzzled by the nature of the resurrection body. Is it the same body that died? Paul makes it clear that there is a

68

relationship between the body that is buried and that which rises; just as there is an intimate relationship between the seed that is sown and the plant which results. The new body must be different from the old in that it is fashioned so as to be suitable to its new environment. The relationship is not that of material identity but of glorified individuality.

(*a*) *The old is sown in Corruption, the new is raised in Incorruption* (v. 42). Our earthly bodies are subject to decay. They belong to the material creation, and are subject to its laws. They are dust and to the dust they return at death. The resurrection body belongs to another order and will not be subject to earthly laws.

(*b*) *The old is sown in Dishonour, the new is raised in Glory* (v. 43). There is nothing more pathetic than a corpse. There is nothing we can do with it but bury it, unless we go to elaborate lengths to preserve it, as the ancient Egyptian did; and there seems to be little point in that. Even our Lord's body was a sad sight as it was laid in the tomb, but His resurrection body was a glorious sight for all who saw it.

(*c*) *The old is sown in Weakness, the new is raised In Power* (v. 43). We are conscious all too often of the weakness of the body. The spirit is willing, when the flesh is weak. After His resurrection our Lord was no longer subject to natural laws. He suddenly appeared, and just as suddenly disappeared. After the resurrection our service will no longer be limited by physical frailty.

(*d*) *The old is sown a Natural Body, the new is raised A Spiritual Body* (v. 44). This is a fact we must never forget. Far too often we are inclined to think of the resurrection body in terms of these physical bodies we now have, forgetting that they are fashioned to suit this earthly and temporal environment. Further in our description of the resurrection body we cannot go.

3. *THE POWER WHICH MAKES SUCH A RESURRECTION POSSIBLE* vv. 45–57

Inevitably we ask, how is such a resurrection possible? The answer is clear.

(*a*) *It is possible through Christ* (v. 45). He is the last Adam, and the apostle describes Him as 'a quickening spirit'. The body can do no other than sink into its own element. Christ is the Lord who came down from heaven. He came down from heaven that He might raise us to heaven.

(b) *It is effected by the return of Christ* (vv. 51–52). Paul refers to this return as a mystery, something that has not been hitherto revealed. Christ's coming for the church was a truth that could not be revealed until the church had been established. The reference to the 'last trump' (v. 52) is an allusion to the Roman army. There were three trumpet calls. The first was 'strike tents', the second 'fall in', and the third and last 'move away'.

4. *THE RESURRECTION CARRIED WITH IT A CHALLENGE* v. 58

It constitutes a challenge to the Christian. A challenge to be,

(a) *resolute*, or 'steadfast'. Dr. G. Campbell Morgan maintains that it refers to personal faithfulness.

(b) *reliable*, or 'immovable'.

(c) *resourceful*, 'always abounding'. It is the hope which should ever keep us active in the work of the Lord.

1 CORINTHIANS 16. 1–24

Closing Remarks

Closing remarks are often important and certainly must not be ignored. Some expositors are of the opinion that these closing words of Paul are wholly personal, and have little or no meaning for us today. Others are as confident that this passage is concerned with practical directions. It is certainly personal. Paul conveys his greetings and indicates his plans, but it is also full of practical directions. History always has its lessons to teach us, and we can learn much from the lives of men like Paul. We can safely say that this final chapter is both personal and practical.

1. There is *A PRINCIPLE WE CAN APPLY* vv. 1–2

Paul called upon the church in Corinth to join with other churches in contributing towards the needs of the saints in Jerusalem. The early churches were bound together by the bonds of Christian love. They had a mutual responsibility one towards another. When we are asked to give, inevitably questions arise. Here Paul answers them.

(*a*) *Why should we give?* For the churches in Galatia there was an apostolic command. Paul wrote, 'I have given order'. Paul's order was backed by Divine authority. Israel were commanded to give a tithe. As we receive so we must give.

(*b*) *When should we give?* 'Upon the first day of the week' (v. 2) they were to give, when they came to worship; when they came to remember the Lord's death. There is not a better moment to give, than when we remember what He has given for us. The first day was that of the open tomb. That is the time for the open purse.

(*c*) *How shall we give?* Paul makes four things clear in verse 2:

  i. We must give personally. 'Everyone of you.'
 ii. We must give proportionally. 'As God hath prospered Him.'
iii. We must give preparedly. 'Lay by him in store.'
 iv. We must give purposely. 'That there be no gatherings when I come.'

Paul was anxious to avoid any hasty collections taken on his arrival. Nothing is more embarrassing. If we were to heed this principle of giving, then our church finances would never be at a low ebb. We should not be driven to take questionable expedients to raise money.

2. There are *THE PLANS THE APOSTLE MAKES*

Paul wrote this letter while at Ephesus. He intended visiting Corinth by way of Macedonia. There is nothing wrong in making plans. We all need to make plans. Being active in God's work does not mean that we sit or stand by passively waiting until God suddenly reveals His plans. It is essential that we look for the opportunities; the 'open door' (v. 9) as Paul calls it.

However, Paul was very conscious that he was in the Lord's hand, and that he must never depart from the Lord's will. That is why he adds the phrase, 'if the Lord permit'. Paul uses the phrase, 'I will' repeatedly in this passage, but it is always conditioned by a will superior to his. When we make our plans in the Lord's service, let us never forget they must be subject to His will.

3. We have *PARTNERS IN OUR WORK*

Paul mentions two of his partners, Timothy and Apollos. How different they were! Timothy was as yet a young inexperienced servant: Apollos was the silver tongued orator who had been led to Christ by Aquila and Priscilla. It reminds us that there is a place for all in the Lord's service. We cannot serve the Lord alone, we need the help of others; we must learn to work with others. Paul took every opportunity to associate others with him in the gospel.

4. There are *PRECEPTS WHICH WE MUST ALL OBEY*

(*a*) *There is a command to watch and stand fast in the faith* (v. 13). This is the kind of command that a general gives to his troops. In the warfare against evil there is need for constant vigil and courage.

(*b*) *There is a command to love* (v. 14). This is a quality which we have seen is essential in our Christian work. If there had been more love in Corinth, there would have been less dissension.

(*c*) *There is a command to submit* (v. 16). No organisation can function without discipline and authority. Alas, often we feel that the church is the place where every man may do that which he pleases. If the church is to be effective, then we must submit ourselves to those who are over us in the Lord. It is humbling to the flesh, but it is glorifying to God.

Summary of 2 Corinthians

THE PURPOSE OF THIS EPISTLE

(*a*) To express the apostle's joy over the repentance of the Corinthian Christians.

(*b*) To reprove those within the church who were still rebellious

(*c*) To reason with those who denied his apostolic status.

THE TIME AND PLACE OF ITS WRITING

It was probably written in A.D. 56 or 57 from Macedonia (vide the note on Paul's Corinthian correspondence).

AN ANALYSIS OF THE EPISTLE

I Salutation (1.1–7)

II A Call for Consideration on the Part of the Corinthian Christians (1.8–5.21)

    i. An explanation of Paul's delay in visiting them (1.8–24)
    ii. A revelation of Paul's purpose in writing to them (2.1–17)
    iii. A manifestation of Paul's message when preaching to them (3.1–18)
    iv. A declaration of Paul's suffering in ministering to them (4.1–18)
    v. A contemplation of Paul's hope as fellow Christians with them (5.1–21)

III A Call for Consecration by the Corinthian Christians (6.1–9.15)

    i. A call which involves separation unto the Lord (6.1–18)

ii. A call which involves cleansing through repentance from the Lord (7.1–16)
iii. A call which involves self-sacrifice for the Lord (8.1–24)
iv. A call which involves a sense of stewardship before the Lord (9.1–15)

IV A Call for Co-operation (10.1–13.10)

i. On account of Paul's authority over them (10.1–18)
ii. On account of Paul's affection for them (11.1–33)
iii. On account of Paul's affliction for them (12.1–21)
iv. On account of Paul's admonition of them (13.1–10)

V A Final Appeal and Blessing (13.11–14)

2 CORINTHIANS I. 1–2

Spiritual Relationships

The salutation at the commencement of this second epistle is, as we should expect, similar to that which opens the first, but we may treat it in a different way. We may concentrate our attention more closely upon the terms which are employed to describe the personnel involved. It is most illuminating for us to study the terms which are used to define believers. Jesus called His disciples 'Friends' (John 15.13, 14). We learn from the Acts that early Christians were known to the authorities as 'People of the Way' (Acts 9.2), and we are informed that the term 'Christian', with which we are so familiar was employed first in Antioch (Acts 11.26). In these opening verses of the second epistle to the Corinthians four terms are used, applicable to us as Christian believers.

1. Paul refers to himself as *AN APOSTLE OF JESUS CHRIST BY THE WILL OF GOD*

It is true of course that in a limited sense there are no apostles today; yet, in the wider sense of the term, every Christian is an

74

apostle. In classical Greek it was used to denote either an individual or a naval expeditionary force, usually the former. An apostle, to a Greek-speaking Jew was a special messenger, employed on some religious mission. To the Christian church an apostle was,

(a) *a witness of the resurrection.* We may all claim to be such as Paul did, since, by faith we too have had a vision of the Risen Christ. We have met Him upon our Damascus Road, and He has radically changed our lives.

(b) *one who knew and experienced the truth of the gospel.* We too have shared this knowledge and experience. We mediate the truth of the gospel to others through life and lip.

(c) *one who possessed superhuman power.* Apostles were expected to work miracles. We may not be able to perform miracles in the name of the Lord, but we are possessed with the supernatural power of the Spirit of God. We can all be 'more than conquerors' through Christ. Every Christian should realise his apostolic commission.

2. Paul refers to Timothy as *A BROTHER*

If the term 'apostle' reminds us of our Divine commission, then the term 'brother' reminds us of our spiritual relationship with others through Christ. The term carries with it a reminder of,

(a) *Privilege.* It suggests a family relationship. For us as Christians it involves knowing God as our Father, since we are 'born . . . of God' (John 1.13). We can pray saying, 'Our Father, which art in heaven. . . .' It means too, that we are the brethren of all who have shared the experience of the new birth.

(b) *Responsibility.* Privilege always carries with it responsibility. If we are brethren, then we are 'our brother's keeper'. Their needs are ours, their cares are ours. Do we not often employ the term 'brother' far too lightly, without any consciousness of the implications involved?

3. Paul refers to God's people in Corinth as *THE CHURCH OF GOD*

The church is God's. He has chosen it, He has purchased it for Himself. He is fashioning it to His own design. He in time will consummate it. We think of the church as an earthly instrument, let us never forget that it is a Divine organism.

4. Paul employs the term *SAINTS*

The term means 'holy ones', those who have been set apart for God. The fundamental idea is that of separation from evil unto God. Alas, separation has been often confused with isolation. Separation in the scriptural sense is distinctiveness. This is the function of 'grace and peace', grace to restore and peace to make us a redemptive force in society.

2 CORINTHIANS I. 3-4

A Cause for Praise

'Blessed be God.' Why this paean of praise? It is on account of God's comfort. Comfort is a word much misunderstood. To most it means that which soothes and softens, its Latin derivation however suggests strength. In our tribulation and trouble it is strength we so sorely need. There are three aspects of this Divine comfort we do well to notice.

I. *ITS SOURCE*

God is the source of all comfort. When Paul writes about God, he was not thinking of any of the pagan deities familiar to the Corinthians, but the God of his fathers, the God who had revealed himself in the Old Testament scriptures, and most of all, the God who had revealed Himself supremely in Jesus Christ.

(a) *The God, whom Jesus called 'Father'*, the God whom Jesus

76

taught His disciples to call 'Father'. Jesus called God, Father, because of His own intimate filial relationship with God. Truly Jesus was uniquely THE Son of God, but we are all sons of God through the new birth. We should enjoy an intimate filial relationship with God.

(b) *The God, who is 'the Father of all mercies'*. Here we see Paul's Hebrew background manifesting itself. To the Jew God was the God of mercy, that is, a compassionate God who specialised in mercy, whose heart went out in love towards His creatures. How good to be reminded that

> 'There is no place where earth's sorrows
> Are felt more than up in heaven'!

(c) *The God, who is the God of all comfort*, that is, the God who is the source of all strength. We are weak apart from Him. When we lay hold upon God, we lay hold upon the power which created and sustains the universe.

2. *ITS SCOPE*

There is no limitation to the 'comfort of God'.

(a) *It is all embracing in its scope*. Notice the word 'all'. How often we are tempted to think that there is some sphere of trouble where God is unable to enter: some trial which is so intimately our own, so remote from the experience of others, even God has no place in it.

(b) *It is continuous in its operation*. Paul employs the present tense purposely. Alas, human sympathy, however sincere, is so transient. Our sorrow is so soon forgotten by others, but never by God.

(c) *It is both personal and communal in its nature*. We must mark Paul's use of the personal pronouns, 'us' and 'our' in verse 3. The apostle was not writing merely about the tribulation of himself and Timothy, but those of the Corinthians too. He is writing collectively. He is at one with these believers communally. 'The collective experience of affliction is sustained by the collective experience of comfort.'

3. ITS SERVICE

If we receive comfort, it is that we may comfort others. Our strength is to be shared, not selfishly indulged in. God often permits us to experience sorrow, so that we may comfort others in their time of sorrow.

2 CORINTHIANS 1. 5-6

Suffering and Serving

The service of God meant suffering for our Master; it is bound to mean suffering for us. Jesus left His disciples in no doubt as to the cost of discipleship. He clearly revealed that it meant a cross. We think of Christianity in terms of salvation and rightly so. But salvation carries with it implications. It means that we must suffer with Him, we must be prepared to bear the agony of the Saviour. There are three points we must note in these two verses, and this is the first of them.

1. WE MUST SHARE CHRIST'S SUFFERING FOR THE WORLD

This of course does not mean that we can be its sin bearer in the way Christ was, but it does mean, we must share His heartache with Him. We must notice how he bore the sorrows of mankind.

(a) *When He fed the hungry multitude, He not only realised their physical need – a point which the disciples only saw – he realised their spiritual need as well.* He saw them 'as sheep without a shepherd'. We must 'look on the crowd as the Master looked, till our eyes with tears grow dim'.

(b) *When He stood at the grave of Lazarus, He wept, because He felt the pain of human sorrow.* He knew the heartbreak of Martha and Mary.

'In every pang that rends the heart
The man of Sorrows has a part.'

(*c*) *He knew the pain which ostracism brings.* He was deserted by His friends. He was so often misunderstood, even by those nearest to Him. How he must have felt with the leper and the woman suffering from the issue of blood, ostracised as they were from society!

(*d*) *He groaned at men's unbelief.* Alas we take modern indifference for granted, and often content ourselves with the knowledge that we are saved, but show no concern for those who are still outside of the kingdom.

2. *WE MUST BRING COMFORT THROUGH CHRIST TO THE WORLD*

We must not miss the two little words in verse 5 'as . . . so'. This means,

(*a*) *That according to the measure we suffer with Christ for men, we are enabled to comfort men through Christ in their sufferings.* Those who have been the greatest service to God have been those who have suffered most for Him.

(*b*) *This comfort we experience and share with others is more than ample for every circumstance.* Note the word 'aboundeth'. How often in our pastoral work we feel hopelessly inadequate to comfort the sorrowing and distressed!

(*c*) *We must never forget that this comfort can only be ours, both in our own sorrow, and through us to others in their sorrow, 'by Christ'.* Human sympathy however rich and deep it may be, is a poor substitute for the comfort of God, which is ours in Christ.

3. *WE MUST BE PREPARED TO ENDURE SUFFERING AND ENJOY COMFORT AS AN EXAMPLE IN THE WORLD* v. 6

Someone stands because we have stood in some difficult situation. Someone endures because we have endured before them. We are to be stepping stones for others, and let us never forget that stepping stones are of no use whatsoever unless they are trodden underfoot. Let us be prepared to be trodden underfoot that others might pass over some stream of suffering.

The Secret of a Firm Faith

In these verses Paul refers to the tribulation he and his companions had suffered. He did so not to excite sympathy for himself (Paul never yielded to the mood of self pity as we often do), but so that others in Corinth might be encouraged by reason of his endurance. How can we stand firm in the midst of trial and temptation? This is a pertinent question, which every Christian must ask at some time. The answer is here.

1. There must be *A GENUINE INTEREST IN THE WELFARE OF OTHERS* v. 7

The motto of the Christian must never be 'self first', not even in times of tribulation. The secret of victorious Christian living is of course God first, and others next in order of priority. In spite of his own trials and tribulation, Paul was primarily concerned about the spiritual state of the Corinthian believers. Notice the phrase in verse 7, 'for you' (R.V.). In spite of all that he had heard concerning the sad spiritual state of the church in Corinth his hope for them was steadfast. Why was this?

(a) *Because in suffering they had stood firm.* The apostle knew that where there was suffering in any Christian community there would be those who would stand firm, some to the extent of becoming martyrs. It is significant that our English word 'martyr' is derived from the Greek verb 'to witness'. Where there was suffering, then the apostle knew that there would be witness for the Lord Jesus Christ, and nothing encouraged him more than this.

(b) *Because in suffering he knew they would be strengthened.* He was confident that suffering brought with it strength. The limbs of the athlete may be sore with training, but the soreness is a sign of increasing strength. The association of trial and Divine strength is to be found also in Matt. 5.4; 2 Tim. 2.12; 1 Pet. 5.10.

80

(*c*) *Because too, in their suffering, they had been encouraged by his own example*. The suffering of Paul and his companions had been exceptionally intense (vv. 8–9). It is possible for God to allow us to pass through suffering, even intense suffering, in order that others may be helped by our courage and endurance.

2. There must be *A LACK OF TRUST IN OUR OWN RESOURCES* v. 9

Paul had discovered that the purpose of his intense suffering was to throw him wholly upon God. This is clear from his words in verse 8, 'we were pressed out of measure, above strength', or as it may be better translated, 'we were weighed down exceedingly beyond our power'. The contrast here is between human weakness and divine power (see verse 9). Human weakness is the experience of us all. Divine Power is the vital need of every believer.

3. There must be *A FIRM CONFIDENCE IN GOD* vv. 9–10

There is every reason why our faith should be firmly planted in God.

(*a*) *He is the God of resurrection* (v. 9). The resurrection is the vindication of God's power. There is no greater power than that which restores life from death.

(*b*) *He is the God of emancipation* (v. 10). He is the God who delivers. As He has delivered in the past, so He will deliver in the future.

(*c*) *He is the God of supplication* (v. 10). He is the God who hears and answers our prayers. We can have fellowship in prayer before the throne of Grace. Could there be any greater ground of confidence than this?

The Secret of Inward Joy

It is true that the Christian life involves suffering. Certainly we must expect trials and tribulations, but joy must ever be an essential element in the Christian experience. We must distinguish between joy and happiness. Happiness depends, as the word suggests, upon what happens. It may be superficial. Joy is undisturbed by changing circumstances. It is like the unruffled depths of the ocean. Here Paul refers to 'our rejoicing'. The question inevitably arises, 'How can we experience inward joy?'

1. *THE TESTIMONY OF A GOOD CONSCIENCE*
v. 12

Where there is a disturbed conscience there cannot possibly be any inward joy. John makes this clear in his first epistle (1 John 1.4–9). Paul makes it clear that a good conscience involves three factors.

(*a*) *Simplicity*, or 'holiness', which is probably preferable since this is the reading of several MSS. Whatever may be our particular theories on scriptural holiness, we are all agreed there is a need in practice for holiness of life. How much joy would be radiated if there was more holiness among Christians!

(*b*) *Sincerity*. Notice that Paul writes of 'godly sincerity', that is, a sincerity which is derived from God. Unbelievers are often the sincerest people in the world. Sincerity is not peculiar to Christians, but sincerity derived from God is. We can be sincerely wrong, but not if we are Christians directed by the Spirit and the Word of God.

(*c*) *Serenity*. This is the outcome of the abandonment of fleshly wisdom and the reception of divine grace (v. 12). We have seen that in the salutation at the commencement of the epistles, grace is associated with peace. They are always associated in experience. If we are enjoying the grace of God then we shall have the testimony of a good conscience; we shall live our lives experiencing continually God's peace which 'passeth all understanding'.

2. FRANKNESS IN OUR FELLOWSHIP WITH OTHERS

Paul was not guilty of gossiping about the Corinthian believers (see v. 13). There is nothing which destroys fellowship quicker than gossip. Often however, fellowships are disrupted because there is an absence of Christian frankness. Paul points to four vital needs of every Christian community in these verses. We do well to mark them.

(a) *The need for openness in conversation.* We can be and should be frank, without being malicious and hurtful. We must speak the truth, but let us never forget that we must 'speak the truth in love'. The Church that is smothered with the cloak of social politeness will never be an effective witness for the Lord.

(b) *The need for mutual acknowledgement of debt.* Paul in his Roman epistle acknowledged his debt to the Greeks and to the Barbarians. Here he acknowledges the fact that he glories in their faith, even as they gloried in what he had done among them. It is as we realise ourselves as a community of God's people that we rejoice in the ministry of the church.

(c) *The need for confidence in each others word* (vv. 17–20). Our word as Christians should be as God's word to us, not 'yea and nay', or as we might say, 'one thing and another', but an utterance which can be relied upon. Where there is distrust, there can be no delight.

3. THE ASSURANCE OF DIVINE ACCEPTANCE

Where there is no assurance, there can be no joy. Joy however is ours because it is God who,

(a) *Seals us with His Spirit* (v. 22). A seal is a sign of ownership, and a mark of authority.

(b) *Secures our future* (v. 22). An earnest is a pledge, usually a sum of money paid, that is, a deposit. The possession of the Holy Spirit is a deposit which not only assures us that we are God's, but that our future is with God.

(c) *Witnesses our service* (vv. 23–24). We can call upon God as our witness, and there is no better. His eye sees all. He knows our sincerity. We can stand only through faith in Him. Our reputation is dependent upon him. Nothing brings us more satisfaction than to know that we are respected and revered by others. This should be so. As Christians we know that we are respected and revered, not because of what we are by nature, but because of our standing through grace.

2 CORINTHIANS 2. I–II

The Secret of Communal Joy

Joy is something essentially personal, it is certainly not an abstraction. It is something more than a mere idea or concept. It is more than a philosophical principle. It belongs to the realm of experience, it is an emotion or feeling. Because of this, it may often be inexplicable, but this does not mean it is invalid. Because it is personal it can be shared by others. Indeed it is an essential element in fellowship. Inevitably the question arises, 'How can we experience joy in our communal life?' The answer is to be found in these verses.

1. There must be *MUTUAL TRUST* v. 3

Paul writes of 'having confidence' in the Corinthian believers, that his personal joy might become a communal joy. Paul had opponents in Corinth but he respected their sincerity, and that sincerity was a basis for confidence in them. The apostle knew that if there was mutual trust even, though differences of opinion, there could be mutual joy.

Certainly their divisions had caused him sorrow. He was sorry that the assertion of his apostolic authority had been misunderstood in Corinth. There had been enough sorrow. Sorrow can so easily escalate. He wished to bring it to an end and replace sorrow by joy. How could this be done? First there had to be mutual trust and confidence. How this word of Paul's must have allayed the

84

fears of many in Corinth! If he had written 'having confidence in some', then sorrow would have continued, but that little word 'all' was so reassuring. It cheered the heart of the Corinthian Church, it brought a smile to the faces of the Corinthian believers. Immediately it must have disarmed many of his opponents and paved the way for a peaceful settlement. Truly 'the soft answer turneth away wrath', and most certainly there can be no possibility of communal joy apart from mutual confidence.

2. There must be *DIVINE LOVE* vv. 4, 8

In verse 4 Paul writes of his love for them, while in verse 8, we read of their love for the erring brother. It is significant that the word Paul uses for 'love' is *agape*, the term which is employed to express Divine love, as opposed to brotherly love. Here we should expect him to use the latter, but far from it. He is seeking to bring home to these Corinthian believers that it is Divine love shed abroad in our hearts by the Holy Spirit, which fuses us into a fellowship of joy. We may find human love very limited, we may find that it fails under pressure, but the love which God has planted in our hearts by His Spirit is His own essence, and will never fail. We are linked together by the golden chain of Divine love, 'The love to you' (v.4) and 'Your love toward him'(v. 8).

3. There must be *IMPLICIT OBEDIENCE* v. 9

Paul is not writing here of our personal obedience to the Lord, but our obedience to the principles which he had laid down to them in his previous correspondence. Here it is obedience to principle it must be noted, not obedience to laws. This is where Christianity differs from Judaism. The basis of Judaism was the Mosaic law. The Pharisees had accepted the rabbinical principles as binding. Righteousness, as Paul knew from his own personal experience, lay in the keeping of both law and precepts. Christianity does not offer laws to be obeyed, but principles to be applied. This of course entails obedience, but not obedience to the letter of a law, rather to the guiding Spirit of God. The new commandment is love, love which as we have seen is shed abroad by the Spirit of God.

4. There must be *SINCERE FORGIVENESS* v. 7

This inevitably follows. Where there is love for one another, where life is guided by obedience to principles based on love; then, there will be a genuine concern for the welfare of others, especially those who have sinned, and been subjected to the discipline of the church. How solicitous we are about the unfortunates of the world, yet alas, how hard and unforgiving in spirit towards those whom we deem to have brought dishonour upon our fellowships by their sin! How many such are allowed to drift from Christian fellowship completely, and are lost to the service of the Lord, where genuine forgiveness would have led to the prodigal's repentance and return.

2 CORINTHIANS 2. 12–13

The Open Door

The 'door' is a familiar obect to us all. It is frequently referred to figuratively in scripture (vide Gen. 4.7; Ps. 141.3; Hos. 2.15; Rev. 3.20; 4.1). Our Lord applied the figure to Himself (John 10.7, 9). Paul uses it also in 1 Cor. 16.9 and Col. 4.3 in either the same or a similar sense to its use here in his second Corinthian epistle. Obviously it means an entrance or way of access, although in Rev. 4.1 it may possibly indicate the commencement of a new era. We may interpret it as 'Opportunity'. We notice three things.

1. *THE CHALLENGE OF THE OPEN DOOR*

Paul's one concern was to spread the Gospel. It was while he was engaged in this all important business, that he found an open door. We cannot expect to find openings for preaching the gospel unless we make it our business to go forth and preach it. Doors open when we take the initiative. Both Wesley and Whitefield discovered this when they took to 'field' or open air preaching, at a time when many of the church doors of England were closed to them. What is the nature of this challenge?

86

(*a*) *We must notice that it is 'of the Lord'* (v. 12). Not every door that opens is 'of the Lord', but we can be sure that whenever a door is opened for the preaching of the gospel it is 'of the Lord'. We are right ever to seek the Lord's will, but we must remember that the preaching of the gospel is always according to His will.

(*b*) *We must mark too that it was a door opened 'by the Lord'.* There are many doors that would remain fast closed against us if it were not for the Lord. Missionaries have discovered this repeatedly. How often there is some miraculous turn of events which changes the whole situation in which we find ourselves! This is not 'luck' or 'chance' but the sovereign act of God.

(*c*) *Let us not miss the fact that it is 'for the Lord'.* The door of opportunity is opened in order that we may witness for Christ. So often we treat the open door as a means of publicising ourselves. It is not God's intention that we should talk about ourselves, but rather we should proclaim Christ,

> 'Our every sacred moment spend,
> Publishing the sinner's friend.'

2. THE CHRIST OF THE OPEN DOOR

We cannot miss Paul's emphasis upon Christ. The gospel is described as His. The door is opened 'of Him'. We cannot read these words without thinking of the figure as applied by our Lord to Himself.

(*a*) *It is through this door we go FOR CHRIST.* For Paul there was always a sense of urgency about his mission (vide Rom. 12.11; 1 Cor. 7.29; 2 Cor. 6.2). In Eph. 5.16 and Col. 4.5 he writes of 'redeeming the time', which phrase Dr. Weymouth translated as 'buying up your opportunities'. When we go for Christ we must move swiftly through the open door, while the opportunity is presented to us.

(*b*) *It is through this door we go WITH CHRIST.* The Lord never sends us anywhere alone. His last word to His disciples before His ascension as He gave them the great commission was, 'Lo, I am with you always'. So often we tremble on the threshold, fearing to take up the challenge, but we can be assured of His presence as we proclaim His gospel.

87

(c) It is through this door we go TO CHRIST, not in the sense of death but in service. It is as we serve Him, as we take up the challenge of the opportunities presented to us by Him that we are brought closer to him. We cannot expect to live in close communion with Him unless we are prepared to obey and serve Him. The door of service brings us into intimate fellowship with Him.

3. *THE CLOSURE OF THE OPEN DOOR*

Verse 13 presents a striking and sad contrast to that which immediately precedes it. We feel that we must supply the word 'but' to link the two verses. It appears that Paul was not able to take advantage of the open door at Troas in the way he would have wished. He was troubled when he did not find Titus as he had expected. We must not condemn Paul for this, rather it is to his credit he was so concerned for his brother's welfare. Yet how often this is the case. There stands before us the open door, but we are not able through circumstances to take full advantage of the opportunity to preach the gospel, as we would wish. How vital it is that we see the open doors and enter them for the Lord whenever it is possible.

2 CORINTHIANS 2. 14–17

The Character of the Christian Life

It is understandable that at times we should be troubled in spirit as Paul was, when on his arrival at Troas he did not find Titus awaiting him. The apostle was eager to hear from Titus the effect his severe letter had had on the church in Corinth. All who bear the burdens of others must expect to be troubled as the apostle was. Troubling however can, and should, issue in triumph. God promised that Achor, the place of Israel's troubling (Jos. 7.26) would become for them 'a door of hope' (Hos. 2.15). Christ makes all the difference to our lives. The Christian life is distinctive because of Christ. How clearly this is expressed in the closing verses of this chapter! We may notice three characteristics of the Christian life.

1. *IT IS A LIFE TRIUMPHANT IN CHRIST*
v. 14

We may be troubled but we can be triumphant over trouble. No doubt Paul had in mind the spectacle of a Roman triumph, when victor and vanquished paraded in the sight of all the city. Like his Master, Paul had come forth victorious over all difficulties, leading captivity captive. This triumphant life is so vital for us all. We need to inquire more closely into its nature. Mark how Paul describes it.

(a) *A constant experience.* Notice the word 'always'. Those who win wars are confident of the ultimate issue even in times of defeat. Winston Churchill never thought in terms of defeat even when hard pressed by the enemy, and Franklin D. Roosevelt was determined the U.S.A. would triumph even when the news of Pearl Harbour shattered American morale. We can triumph not merely over trouble, but in trouble.

(b) *A God-directed experience.* The phrase, 'causeth us to triumph' should be translated 'leadeth us in triumph'. Paul recognised that the honour was not his, but God's. It is God who heads the triumphal procession. Paul follows as an officer in His army, sharing in His victory. Alas, so often in our moments of success we forget that the victory is God's. We plead for His help in moments of difficulty but ignore Him when the victory is won.

(c) *A Christ-empowered experience.* Paul makes it crystal clear that this triumph is 'in Christ', that is, through our union with Him. God's power flows to us through Christ. It is only as we realise our intimate relationship with Christ, that we can enjoy the victory God intends for us.

2. *IT IS A LIFE GLORIOUS FOR CHRIST*
vv. 14b–15

A triumphal procession was accompanied by the burning of incense. This is the allusion here. The thanks are due to God

89

(v. 14) and we are 'unto God' the fragrance of Christ, but the fragrance is Christ. The Christian life must exude Christ, because it is Christ, Christ dwelling in the heart of the believer. What does Christ in us mean? The answer is to be found here.

(*a*) *It is the spread of knowledge of Christ by us.* Just as the smell of the incense pervaded the streets during the triumphal procession, so the knowledge of Christ was pervading the whole of the Roman world, through the witness of the apostles. If we are to bring glory to Christ then we must spread the knowledge of Him to those who are still living in ignorance of the truth of the gospel.

(*b*) *It is the judgement of Christ through us* (vv. 15–16). The smell of the incense was life; triumphant life indeed, to the victor, but death to the vanquished. Nothing annoyed the Roman persecutor of the Christians more than the confidence with which they faced death in the arena. The savour of Christ was abhorrent to those who were not Christ's. The true Christian exposes the corruption of the world around him, but at the same time he manifests the light and life of Christ within him. The saints are already judging the world by the saintliness of their lives.

3. *IT IS A LIFE ELOQUENT OF CHRIST* v. 17

We must not miss the phrase 'in the sight of God speak we in Christ'. Many were dealing deceitfully with the gospel in Paul's day by lowering its standards. The same is true in many quarters today, in an age of declining standards. How imperative it is therefore, that Christians should speak of Christ, plainly knowing that at the judgement bar of God they must answer for the message they have declared!

2 CORINTHIANS 3. 1–4

The Open Letter

The character of Paul's ministry was accredited by the Corinthian Christians themselves. Paul had brought the gospel to Corinth in the first place. He had been the instrument of their conversion. They were his letter of commendation. Early Christians, when travelling from one church to another, carried with them letters of introduction or 'commendation' as they were called. These letters were secret missives between churches, but the lives of the Corinthian Christians were open letters, which could be read by all men. This was a sobering truth they had forgotten. Paul hastens to remind them of this fact. It is a truth none of us must forget. It is challenging to think of ourselves as letters or epistles.

1. Firstly, we must consider the truth itself, *WE ARE EPISTLES*

By this, Paul meant letters of commendation. The missives which Christians carried with them from one church to another, commended them as Christian believers of upright character, who could be received into the fellowship of the local church. Inevitably the question arises 'Do we commend Christ?' This question is so vital because,

(a) *We are OPEN LETTERS* (v. 2). We are read of all men. Men may take little notice of what we say. They may not enter our church doors to listen to our sermons, or pause to heed the message declared in the open air, but they take notice of what we are, and how we behave. They see sermons enacted when they will not hear them preached. We are open for all the world to see.

(b) *We are OPEN LETTERS OF CHRIST* (v. 3). Though the Corinthian believers were Paul's letters of commendation (v. 2), Christ was the author of these letters. Paul was but the scribe employed to dictate the Divine message upon the parchment of their lives. We are not in the world to commend any organisation or individual, nor to commend some denomination or preacher, but to commend Christ. He is the author of our life. Those who have helped us in the Christian life are but His scribes.

(c) *We are OPEN LETTERS OF CHRIST WRITTEN BY OTHERS*. While it is Christ's honour that is first and foremost at stake, we have a responsibility to those who have been Christ's scribes. We must never lose sight of the instruments and agencies which have brought us to Christ, and directed us along the Christian pathway. As others have helped us, so we too must offer ourselves as Christ's scribes, that His message may be written upon the lives of others.

2. Secondly, we must notice that *WE ARE EPISTLES WRITTEN WITHIN*

Mark that Paul does not use the preposition 'on' but 'in' (vv. 2, 3); openly manifested to the world but embedded deep in the experience of the heart. This means

(*a*) *Our expression is not an external façade but an internal force.* The Law given to Moses was written on tables of stone, which were laid up in the ark of the covenant. Not so the gospel, it is experienced by the heart, but revealed openly to the world.

(*b*) *Our expression is not merely knowledge of Christ's word, but a living experience of Christ's power.* The heart to the Hebrew was the seat of knowledge, as the mind is to us. To us the heart signifies emotion and feeling. Thought of course arouses feeling. The phrase 'in the heart' means an emotional experience of power.

(*c*) *Our expression is not merely the result of an internal impression, it is the manifestation of a converted heart.* Our Lord declared that it is out of the heart of man evil comes (Matt. 15.18). Jeremiah said, 'The heart is deceitful above all things and desperately wicked' (Jer. 17.9). It is the changed heart which is revealed to men.

3. Thirdly, we must notice that *WE ARE EPISTLES WRITTEN WITH THE INK OF THE SPIRIT*

Ink fades, but not so the Spirit of God. It is indelible. Paul refers to the Spirit not merely for this reason, but principally because of the work of the Spirit in the life of the believer.

(*a*) *It is the Holy Spirit who reveals Christ to us* (John 16.14).

(*b*) *It is the Holy Spirit who effects Christ's character in us* (Gal. 3.2). The Spirit is life, indeed as Paul points out here, the Spirit of the *living* God. Epistles of God read of all men, what a challenging thought this is!

Divine Sufficiency

Living triumphantly, gloriously and eloquently for Christ, and the thought of being an open letter, read and known of all men might discourage the most eager would-be Christian. Yet it is wonderfully possible, since the power lies not in ourselves, not even in our determination to be what God intends, but in God. 'Our sufficiency is of God' (v.5). Whom God calls into his service He equips. This is Paul's theme here in this section of the chapter. Notice what God offers those who are ready through Christ to live for Him.

1. *A GIFT TO EXERCISE* v. 6

In the teaching profession it is often said that teachers are 'born not made'. It is true that many have a natural ability to communicate truth to others, but the ability to minister God's Word to others is a Divine gift. God calls His men and equips them for His service. He can take a tinker like John Bunyan, just as He called a fisherman like Peter at the beginning of the Christian era. Many characters from the Old Testament too, come to mind, such as Moses, Gideon, David and Amos. When God calls he communicates a special grace (*charisma*). How vividly this is illustrated in the experience of the Old Testament Saul (1 Sam. 10.6, 10, 26)! When Jesus commissioned his disciples to go and make disciples of all nations, He offered them His presence and assured them of His power and authority (Matt. 28.18-20). We can be able ministers, since our sufficiency is of God.

2. *A GOSPEL TO PREACH*

We are ministers of 'the new covenant' (v. 6). God's dealings with Israel were based upon the Covenant made at Sinai. That covenant had been abrogated by Israel's disobedience. Jeremiah (31.31) had foretold a new covenant. Our Lord declared that this new covenant was established through Him. The old covenant was that of law, the new is that of grace. Here Paul draws a threefold contrast between the new and the old.

93

(*a*) *The new covenant is that of a living spirit not a dead letter.*
Israel were never able to keep the old covenant, because of the
sinfulness of human nature. It was a law to be obeyed, a rule to be
observed, an ethic to be lived. Religion for so many is no more
than this. They try their best, and often become exasperated by
their failure. It is no wonder that many give up in despair. To
these folk we can offer not a law to be obeyed, but a life to be
enjoyed.

(*b*) *The new covenant pardons and restores while the old condemns.*
Law cannot save, it can only condemn those who fail to keep it.
This was a favourite theme of the apostle's. The old covenant was
thus a 'ministration of death' (v. 7). Grace through the operation
of the Holy Spirit is a 'ministration of righteousness' (v. 9). While
law reveals our unrighteousness the new covenant imparts
righteousness, so that we are restored to a right relationship with
God.

(*c*) *The new covenant displays a greater glory than anything
hitherto experienced.* The giving of the law and the ratification of
the old covenant at Sinai was undoubtedly a landmark in the
history of religion. It was a glorious moment for mankind, as well
as for Israel. At Sinai, and indeed throughout the Old Testament
era God revealed His glory to His people, but in Christ that glory
has been fully revealed. We now know that God is grace as well as
law. Certainly this was intimated by prophets such as Hosea in
Old Testament times, but now we can say with the writer of the
fourth gospel, 'We beheld His glory, the glory as of the only
begotten of the Father, full of grace and truth' (John 1.14).

3. *A GOAL TO INSPIRE* v. 12

This is indicated by the word 'hope'. There was no hope for a
people who failed to keep God's law. Judgement constantly
hovered over them. That is why the messages of the prophets are so
full of doom. They could alone hope for God's grace. We no
longer need to hope for it, it is ours through Christ. We can look
forward to the future with confidence, knowing that God has
provided a new covenant of grace, a glory now, and an even greater
glory to come. No wonder the apostle declares, 'our sufficiency is of
God'!

94

The Liberty of the Christian

This section begins with an allusion to Moses' descent from Sinai, his face shining with Divine radiance (vide Exod. 34.29–35). It is recorded that Moses veiled his face. We may interpret this as meaning that Moses veiled his face because of the brightness of the shining. Indeed a cursory reading of the Exodus passage plainly suggests this. Paul points out here that Moses veiled his face because the glory was fading, and he did not wish the people to see the fading of that glory. Paul no doubt was eager to point to the law as a fading glory, and those Judaisers who proclaimed it as the gospel were preaching the message of a fading glory. Our gospel is that not of a fading, but an ever increasing glory, since we have turned not to law, but to the Lord (v. 16). The Lord means life through the Spirit, and life means liberty, that is, freedom to live. This is the theme of the writer in these closing verses of the chapter. Inevitably we must inquire into the nature of this liberty.

1. It is *LIBERTY FROM*

Whenever we think of freedom, obviously we imply that there is bondage also. The dualism of thought is inevitable. 'Freedom from what?' we ask. We could answer this question in many ways. We could say and rightly, ours is freedom from the control of Satan, the power of sin, and the domination of self motivation, but it is preferable in expository preaching to adhere as closely as possible to the context of the word. To answer this question therefore we must refer to the previous passage considered (vv. 5–12), as well as the passage now under consideration. What do we discover? We find that this freedom is,

(*a*) *From death* (vv. 6–7). When our Lord died He met the righteous demands of the law. When He rose from the dead He made it possible to live on a far higher level than that of law. We rise from the dust of death with its bondage, into the liberty of life. Paul reminded the Romans that 'the law of the Spirit of life in Christ Jesus hath made me free from the law of sin and death' (Rom. 8.2).

95

(*b*) *From the frustration of law.* Far from providing righteousness for us, our efforts at law keeping only serve to emphasise our unrighteousness. A righteousness has been provided 'apart from the law' (Rom. 3.21). We can truly sing,

> 'Free from the law, O happy condition
> Jesus has bled and there is remission.'

(*c*) *From pessimism* (v. 12). The future formerly offered nothing but the dismal prospect of judgement. Now judgement is passed, we are able to hope, we are free to look forward with optimism. We no longer need to move forward with slow and heavy pace fearing the future but are able to quicken our pace and lighten our step.

2. It is *LIBERTY IN* v.17

Our liberty is in the Lord. We must emphasise the phrases, 'Now the Lord' and 'Where the Spirit of the Lord is'. Our freedom paradoxically comes the moment we submit to His control. Liberty must never be confused with licence, either when thinking of religion or society. In fact licence is a denial of liberty. We are free in Christ.

(*a*) *There is liberty to see clearly* (vv. 13–14). We are no longer blinded as Israel was. Our Lord made it clear that the Spirit will lead men into all truth (John 16.13). There need be no veil either over the eye or the heart of the Christian.

(*b*) *There is liberty to speak plainly* (v. 12). We can be fearless and frank in our testimony. The law was largely negative, the gospel is gloriously positive. The law said, 'Nay' the gospel says 'Yea'.

(*c*) *There is liberty to decide freely.* Paul writes of Israel 'Nevertheless when it shall turn to the Lord' (v. 16). By 'it' Paul means the heart of any unbelieving Jew. Now that grace has been revealed there is no need for anyone to remain in bondage any longer. The shackles have been broken. The Christian sings with Wesley

> 'My chains fell off, my heart was free
> I rose went forth and followed Thee.'

3. It is *LIBERTY FOR*

When Christ emancipates us, it is not that we might please ourselves. This would indeed be licence. We are freed that we might serve Him. It is imperative that those who have been liberated by Him should understand and study His word, and declare it frankly and fully to others. Having turned to the Lord themselves, they should seek to win others for Him.

2 CORINTHIANS 3. 17–18

The Change Christ Brings

The closing verses of this chapter are so full of thought and have such an important message to convey to us, they deserve further consideration and exposition. We can never exhaust the mine of Divine truth; there is always light and truth to break forth from God's Word. Paul here is not only dealing with emancipation, he is concerned also with the transformation which results from union with Christ. 'We are changed', he declares in verse 18. Such a tremendous declaration deserves our serious attention. We may consider this change in three ways as they are suggested to us here.

1. *THE POWER WHICH EFFECTS THIS CHANGE*

We need to notice that Paul attributes our emancipation to the Lord (v. 17). The Lord is the Holy Spirit which is operative in the world convicting and converting. One of the last words Christ uttered before His ascension was, 'Ye shall receive power after that the Holy Spirit is come upon you' (Acts 1.8). We need however to inquire more closely into the nature of this power.

(*a*) *It is an authoritative power*. Paul uses the term 'Lord' which was commonly used in the early church to refer to the Master. He was more than a Rabbi or Teacher, He was their Lord. Now of course a Rabbi was a Master, in that he could speak with authority, but Christ was more than a teacher to the early Christians. By reason of His resurrection He was their Lord (Acts 2.36). Doubting Thomas acknowledged Him as that in the upper room when he said, 'My Lord and my God' (John 20.28). The name of Jesus meant power (vide Acts 4.7, 10).

(b) *It is a Divine power.* Acknowledgement by Paul of the Lordship of Christ was a witness to His deity, as it was with Thomas (John 20.28). No other kind of power could effect conversion in a man's heart and life. We cannot explain conversion wholly by means of psychology. It is a spiritual phenomenon brought about by the Spirit of God. 'We are changed . . . by the Spirit of the Lord' (v. 18).

(c) *It is an available power* (v. 17). 'Where the Spirit of the Lord is. . . .' This does not mean the Spirit of the Lord is confined to some geographical area; it means rather that where the Spirit of the Lord is allowed to operate there is liberty. There is no need for anyone to remain in the bondage of sin, Satan and self. The Spirit of the Lord is available to emancipate every soul who acknowledges his or her need.

2. *THE PROCESS BY WHICH WE ARE CHANGED*

Obviously we are bound to raise the question, 'How can this change be effected in the human heart and life?' The answer is suggested to us here.

(a) *By looking directly to the Lord* (v. 18). The word translated 'open' means unveiled. It suggests looking clearly. To see anything clearly we look directly, or as the photographer would put it 'full faced'. We do not look out of the corner of our eye. We are transformed as we look 'full faced' to the Lord. We look into His eyes and He looks into ours.

(b) *By looking intensely to the Lord.* Paul writes 'as in a glass'. When we look into a glass we do not only look full faced into it, we look intensely into it, to see the details of the reflection. So we must look to Christ if we are to be changed.

(c) *By looking objectively to the Lord.* We must look with a special object in view. We must look to see in particular 'the glory of the Lord'. Dr. G. Campbell Morgan pointed out that here the A.V. rendering is preferable to that of the R.V. 'The idea is not that of reflection in order to transform, but rather that of beholding until transformed in order to reflect.' It is as we concentrate our eyes upon His glory, that we reflect that glory.

3. THE PRODUCT WHICH RESULTS FROM THIS CHANGE

'We are changed into the same image', that is, of course, into Christ's likeness (vide Rom. 12.2; 8.29). Paul employs the present tense indicating that although we are saved the moment we look to the Lord, becoming Christlike is a gradual process. To use Wesley's well-known words:

> 'Changed from glory into glory,
> Till in heaven we take our place,
> Till we cast our crowns before Thee,
> Lost in wonder, love and praise.'

2. CORINTHIANS 4. 1–2

The Christian Ministry

In this chapter Paul continues the theme of his ministry. He was ever conscious of the tremendous responsibility which rested upon him personally, as the apostle to the Gentiles. It is tragically easy for all of us to forget our responsibilities as witnessing Christians, no matter in what capacity we may serve the Master. 'This ministry' (v. 1) is committed to us. With it there are implications. Indeed they are imperatives which we cannot ignore. Three such are indicated here.

1. GOD'S MERCY MUST BE RECEIVED BY US
v. 1

The theme of God's mercy was a favourite of Paul's (see 1 Cor. 7.25; 1 Tim. 1.13.16). Indeed none of us should forget what we owe to Divine mercy. It is a legal term, but it is not so fashionable now as once it was to emphasise the forensic aspect of our salvation. We do well to remind ourselves of what we owe to God's mercy.

(a) *We are spared by God's mercy through Christ.* We deserved not mercy but judgement. Our sin exposed us to Divine wrath, but through the intervention of Christ on our behalf we have been spared. God has dealt with us in mercy. We are debtors to God's mercy. How conscious Paul was of this in his own experience! He thought of himself as 'the chief of sinners'. He had persecuted the church, but God in His mercy had spared him, to carry out 'this ministry'.

(b) *We are secured by God's mercy in Christ.* Because we have been spared, we are secured. Now that we are in Christ, we are justified. Our sin question has been dealt with. 'There is therefore now no condemnation to them which are in Christ Jesus' (Rom. 8.1). We are safe in the shelter of the riven Rock of Ages.

(c) *We are strengthened by God's mercy for Christ.* We do not tremble and faint now that we are spared and secured. God's mercy gives us a confidence we should not otherwise have. In our service for the Master there is no need for any of us to lose heart.

2. FLESHLY EXPEDIENTS MUST BE RENOUNCED BY US   v. 2

It is possible for us to attempt this ministry which God has committed to us in our own power. We can be guilty of trusting 'the arm of the flesh'. If we do, then our ministry will most certainly be ineffective. Paul indicates some of the things which can rob us of our power and make our ministry ineffective.

(a) *Secret sins in the heart* (v. 2). This phrase carries with it the thought of shame. We are ashamed of our secret sins, and try at all costs to hide them from others. It is futile to think that we can hide anything from God. He searches the depths of the hearts,

> 'The chambers where polluted things
> Hold empire oer the soul.'

It is absolutely essential that we bare our hearts before the Lord if we are to be of service to Him.

(b) *An inconsistent walk in the world.* Paul writes about 'walking in craftiness'. If there are secret sins, then there is bound to be an inconsistent walk. Paul's opponents were guilty of this. John writes of walking 'in the light', by which he means a life of consistency as opposed to inconsistency in our witness.

(c) *Handling the word of God in deceit.* Paul here is undoubtedly referring to the Judaisers, who pandered to the Jews by permitting the observance of Jewish laws. It is a warning to us that we can 'water down' the gospel to suit our own purposes. We can pander to the popular taste so as to avoid 'the offence of the gospel'.

3. *DIVINE TRUTH MUST BE REVEALED BY US*

This is the positive aspect of what we have been considering. Our business is to manifest the truth. The English word 'manifest' means literally 'to show one's hand' in the sense in which a conjuror does so to his audience. In preaching the gospel we are to show our hand in the sense we are to keep nothing back from men, but proclaim the whole counsel of God. Notice three points in this connection,

(a) *It is a manifestation to 'every man'.* We must never forget the universality of the gospel appeal. God wills that 'all men be saved and come unto the knowledge of the truth' (1 Tim. 2.4), since 'the grace of God that bringeth salvation hath appeared to all men' (Tit. 2.11).

(b) *It is a manifestation to conscience.* Literally it reads, 'to every kind of conscience'. By this, Paul means that it must have an inward moral response. It is by the fruit of the gospel that the acceptance of its truth is evident.

(c) *It is a manifestation in the sight of God.* Again we find ourselves probing the inner depths of the human heart. So often

101

we successfully deceive ourselves, but we can never deceive God. This is why all must be done under the careful scrutiny of God.

The Hidden Gospel

In verse 3 Paul uses the term 'lost'. It is a word which our Lord employed (Luke 15). The sheep, coin and son were lost. What does it mean? It means that it is hidden from view. Neither coin, sheep, nor son, were to be seen by those who had lost them. But it means more, it means they were perishing. Those who are lost are perishing. The coin was losing its value. Hordes of Roman coins which are frequently found in the once Romanised parts of the British Isles once were valuable, but now they are valueless; they have lost their value, except as antiques. Their value has perished. Obviously the lost sheep and son were perishing. There is a double truth here however, which we must not miss. It is not only that men are lost from sight, but also the gospel is veiled to them. Literally verse 3 reads, 'But if our gospel be hid, it is hid to them that are perishing.' This section is concerned with being lost and found. Indeed this might be chosen as an alternative title.

1. THE IMPLICATIONS OF BEING LOST

We have seen that being lost means being hidden from view and perishing, but it means more.

(a) *We are not able to see the light* (v. 4). The god of this world blinds the eyes of men. Men under Satanic control cannot see any further than the material. They do not have the eye of faith which is able to penetrate the unseen. They are in the dark and are unable to see the light. They are as those whose eyes are covered in a darkened room.

(b) *We are not able to believe God's Word.* Faith is not possible apart from the enlightening power of the Holy Spirit. The gospel is

102

incredible to them, a stumbling block rather than a stepping stone.

(c) *We cannot bear the image of God.* That image has been lost through sin and cannot be restored apart from Christ. God's purpose is that we should be Godlike, that is why at conversion He imparts to us something of His nature. Being lost means being lost to God's likeness.

2. THE METHOD BY WHICH WE ARE FOUND

God has provided a way by which the lost can be restored to Him. We must notice the agencies which are employed.

(a) *Preaching* (v. 5). Paul declares, 'We preach'. In the first epistle he had made it clear that men are being saved through preaching. Preaching might appear to be foolish, indeed it still does to many. So many would far rather observe the spectacle of a ritual than listen to the proclamation of God's word. Sermons are often the subject of ridicule, but none the less it is through the medium of preaching that men are won for God. Faith comes through hearing. If this is to be possible, then there must be preaching.

(b) *Christ-centred preaching.* Not all preaching falls into this particular category. Again and again in Wesley's Journals we read that he came into the cities and towns of England and 'offered them Christ'. Paul's message was not merely that Jesus was Christ or Messiah, but that Jesus was Christ the Lord, Messiah, the Master, who demands our submission.

(c) *The preaching of Christ as Lord by His servants.* 'Ourselves your servants for Jesus' sake.' Paul did not demand submission to himself as some of his accusers maintained, but submission to the Lord. While our message must ever be Christ centred, we must remember that preaching is truth through the medium of human personality. The human personality however is lost sight of in the glory of the Divine. What we do, we do 'for Jesus' sake'.

3. THE PURPOSE OF OUR RECOVERY vv. 6, 7

We have seen that being 'lost', we cannot see the truth of God. God's purpose is that we should. He who is the source of all light, that is, He who brought forth the light at creation by the fiat of His Word, brings light by the same commanding word into our hearts.

This light is knowledge. Not only are we able to see, but in seeing we are able not merely to believe but understand. We can enjoy intelligent faith, and most important of all we can reflect the glory of God in Christ. What a wonderful privilege this is! The lamp which bears the light may be of little value. It is the earthen vessel which contains the oil and the wick, but the light which radiates from the earthen vessel is indeed glorious. God's design for His found ones, is that they be light bearers for Him.

2 CORINTHIANS 4. 8–18

In these verses Paul records the circumstances of his earthly life, what was happening 'on every side' (v. 8). This is what circumstances mean. They are the things, *circum*, around us. We cannot avoid these things. They are beyond our control. We often use the phrase 'under the circumstances', but no Christian should be 'under the circumstances'. They may be around him, but he is able to triumph in spite of them. This surely is the message of these particular verses. In 2.14 we saw that we can enjoy a life triumphant in Christ; here we have a similar yet even more glorious message.

1. TROUBLED, YET TRIUMPHANT THROUGH CHRIST

We are all heirs to trouble, it seems. As the book of Job declares, 'Man is born unto trouble as the sparks fly upward' (Job 5.7). It is no use trying to live an ostrich-like existence with our heads buried in the sand. We must face these troubles. Notice three features of them.

(a) *The extent of them.* 'On every side' (v. 8). An army is prepared to face its enemy on several fronts, but when it faces the enemy on every side it is surrounded. It has little prospect of survival. Its only hope is to break through. The Christian may be surrounded, but he is not defeated.

(b) *The variety of them.* Perplexity (v. 8), persecution (v. 9), pressed down (v. 9). Could there apparently be a worse state of affairs than Paul describes here? We may think our troubles great, but no situation which we may face is so grave as this.

(c) *The victory over them.* Troubled but not distressed, perplexed but not in despair, persecuted but not forsaken, cast down but not destroyed. Often the little word 'but' in scripture introduces a sad story, as in Matt. 14.24, 30. Here it is the reverse. We can thank God for the victory which is possible. No situation is so desperate that God cannot deal with it.

2. *DYING, YET LIVING FOR CHRIST* v. 10

This is an amazing paradox which occurs repeatedly in the New Testament (e.g. Rom. 6; Gal. 2.20). Here the paradox reveals some amazing truths.

(a) *There is a truth which is explained objectively to us.* The mission of Christ was to die. Paul always thought of himself as identified with his Lord. As Christ suffered and died before entering into life beyond the grave, so Paul rejoiced that he should suffer and die to the old self, that he might live the new life, which was his in Christ (vide 1 Cor. 15.31; Rom. 8.36; Phil. 3.10; Col. 1.24).

(b) *There is a truth which is experienced subjectively.* Mark the phrase 'in our mortal flesh' (v. 11). Paul was not writing exclusively about himself. This is an experience which we all must share with him. Often this is thought of as something academic and theological, far remote from actual experience. Far from it, as the children's hymn expresses it,

> 'O day by day each Christian child
> Has much to do without, within;
> A death to die for Jesus' sake
> A weary war to wage with sin.'

(c) This is a truth which is to be expressed ethically through us
Notice the word 'manifest' (vv. 10, 11). The union of the believer
with Christ must result in the manifestation of Christ's life through us
(vide Rom. 8.17; John 14.19). This is the purpose of the suffering,
this is the reason for the dying. Out of death there must issue life.

3. *AFFLICTED TEMPORARILY, YET GLORIFIED ETERNALLY*

The hope which we enjoy is assured by the resurrection of
Christ (v. 14). Like the butterfly we shall emerge gloriously from
this present decaying body (v. 16). Just as the storms smooth the
rocks, so we by our temporal afflictions are being prepared for our
eternal destiny (v. 17). The chapter ends with a reminder that it is
vital for us to have a true perspective as a Christian. If we keep our
eyes upon the temporal and the seen, we shall see no purpose in
all that is happening to us, but if we remember that realities of
life are the unseen, then like Bunyan's pilgrim making for the
Celestial City via the Wicket Gate, we shall keep the light in our
eye as we go forward.

2 CORINTHIANS 5. 1–5

A House not made with Hands

Like many Christians in our own day, Paul and his contemporaries
knew that at any time they might be called upon to seal their
witness in death. It is understandable that the apostle should
consider the possibility, having written about the mortification of
the flesh and the afflictions they faced. What if physical death
should come? Paul had a positive reply to this question.

1. *HE OFFERS THEM AN ASSURANCE* v. 1

We must not miss the certainty with which he writes. 'We
know ... we have.' Neither the A.V. nor the R.V. give the true
106

meaning of Paul's words. The word translated 'building' means permanence and solidity. The word 'house' would have been suitable. 'We know that . . . we have a house of God.' What does this imply?

(*a*) *Strength.* The word building is contrasted with the phrase 'earthly house' which really means a tent. This is made clear by the use of the word 'dissolved', which means 'struck'. A tent is pitched and 'struck' to provide temporary shelter. A house has the quality of strength which is missing in a tent.

(*b*) *That which is supernatural.* 'Not made with hands eternal in the heavens.' Paul does not mean that this mortal body is not of God. Rather, he means that the new resurrection body which awaits us is in every way supernatural. It will not be formed by natural means as is the case with our present bodies.

(*c*) *That which is eternal.* The body is temporal, it is conditioned by time. The heavenly body will partake of the eternal nature of heaven. It will not be subject to disease as this body is. It will not decay, it will not be of 'the earth, earthy' not made of crumbling earth, but an eternal structure of heaven.

2. *HE OFFERS THEM A HOPE*

We might use the word 'prospect'. It is something that we can look forward to. What a blessed prospect it is! It is hope that cheers our earthly path, and inspires us to go forward in faith. This is made abundantly clear in these verses.

(*a*) *Paul suggests that his mortal body may not see physical death* (v. 2). It may be covered with a heavenly body, should the second advent take place before death intervened. This is the thought behind the words 'clothed upon' which literally means 'put on in addition'. In fact Paul yearns for this to happen. This is the meaning of the word translated 'groan'. Paul does not seem to be referring to the frailty of his earthly frame, but rather to his yearning for the heavenly house which he is assured he will receive. This is not a complaint but a cherished hope.

(*b*) *Paul clearly refers to the second advent* (v. 3). Death would mean the separation of soul from body. The soul would be naked.

The apostle shrank from the idea he might be a disembodied spirit. We must remember however that when the soul goes to be with Christ at death, it enters the realm of eternity, and in eternity there is no such phenomenon as the passage of time. For Paul the Lord's return was indeed 'the blessed hope' (Tit. 2.13).

(c) *The hope is that of relief from those burdens which press us down.* The word 'groan' should read 'yearn' or 'sigh'. We do not yearn for death; that would be unnatural and unhealthy. We yearn rather for the heavenly state which follows the second advent of the Saviour. Well may we sing,

'O blessed hope! with this elate,
Let not our hearts be desolate.
But strong in faith, in patience wait
Until He come.'

3. *HE OFFERS THEM A SIGN* v. 5

The very fact that this hope is implanted within our hearts is a sign that God will fulfil His purpose. Whence comes this desire but from Him? 'Wrought' literally means 'worked up' or 'incited'. The presence of the Holy Spirit within us is the assurance that God will surely transform us, giving us a new and heavenly body (vide Eph. 1.14). It is the Holy Spirit who implants Divine life in us. This Divine life must find its consummation in the redemption of the body (vide Rom. 8.9–10).

2 CORINTHIANS 5. 6–10

Absent from the Body, Present with the Lord

Although Paul's earthly life was spent in zealous service for the Lord, and no man looking back across the panorama of the years could find such satisfaction as Paul must have done at the time of his martyrdom, he realised that he could never find full satisfaction on earth. Samuel Rutherford wrote that 'since Christ had run away to heaven with his heart he could never be content anymore on earth'. Engaged as we are so much with earthly concerns, we must never forget that 'our citizenship is in heaven'. This is the point Paul makes here in these verses.

1. *MORTAL EXISTENCE ON EARTH CAN NEVER BE THE GOAL OF THE CHRISTIAN LIFE* vv. 6, 8

In spite of the fact that Paul wrote 'henceforth know we Christ no more after the flesh' (v. 16), one feels that Paul would very much have liked to have been one of the disciple band and experienced the intimate relationship with the Master they enjoyed. We express similar sentiments in our hymns, e.g.

'I think when I read that sweet story of old
When Jesus was here among men,
How He called little children as lambs to His fold,
I should like to have been with them then.
I wish that His hands had been placed on my head,
That His arms had been thrown around me,
And that I might have seen His kind look when He said,
Let the little ones come unto me;'

and

'Jesus these eyes have never seen
That glorious form of thine;
The veil of sense hangs dark between
Thy blessed face and mine.'

For Paul, even though he was indwelt by the Spirit of Christ, Christ was his absent Lord. His soul was so intimately united with Christ it could never find its satisfaction on earth, where there are so many things which hinder our communion. The heart longs to be in the immediate presence of the one it loves, above all else. God has made it that way. It is right therefore, it should desire to be with the Lord.

2. *OUR SPIRITUAL NATURE CRIES OUT FOR FURTHER ACHIEVEMENT*

There is a little of eternity in every life. It is significant that no tribe has been discovered which does not have a religion of some kind, and religion attempts to give an answer to the why and the whither of life. This is particularly true of the Christian and his faith. The saved soul is most conscious of its destiny, and at the same time aware that on earth there must always be something lacking.

(*a*) *Jesus declared His purpose to His disciples*. 'That where I am there ye may be also' (John 14.3). On earth there is spiritual union, in heaven there is an even greater union, the nature of which we cannot fully describe. When we become Christians we are united to Christ, this is the essence of the Christian experience. It is logical that this union should become increasingly greater on earth, finding its consummation in heaven. This consummation involves being 'present with the Lord'.

(*b*) *Paul explains heaven in this beautiful way, 'present with the Lord'*. The apostle implies a further thought in this respect. He writes, that here on earth we are 'at home in the body'; in heaven therefore we shall be 'at home with the Lord'. This thought is in keeping with the words of our Lord referred to above, 'In my Father's house are many mansions. . . . I go to prepare a place for you' (John 14.2). The word translated 'mansions', means 'resting places', such as inns along an eastern road. The final resting place is home. Here our home is a temporary tent, the abode of the pilgrim. Like those who walked to Emmaus (Luke 24.13 ff.) we have Christ with us on the journey, but it is only when we arrive home, that we fully know Him, and He fully reveals Himself to us.

3. *MORTAL EXISTENCE HERE ON EARTH IS CONDITIONED BY FAITH* v. 7

The allusion above is to a journey. The suggestion has been made that life is a pilgrimage. 'We nightly pitch our moving tent a days march nearer home.' Paul writes parenthetically, yet most significantly, 'we walk', and he adds, 'by faith'. Although we move in the realm of the seen, yet we are directed by the unseen.

Columbus travelled on because he firmly believed there were new worlds to be discovered. The scientist labours in his laboratory because he believes there are further discoveries to be made. The sociologist studies society because he is sure society can be improved.

The aircraft cannot see its destination, but is in radio touch with it and directed towards it. So it is with the Christian. We cannot see the end of the road, but we are in touch with home and are being directed towards it.

4. MORTAL EXISTENCE ON EARTH INVOLVES THE ACCEPTANCE OF AN ETHICAL IDEAL
vv. 9, 11

Our aim must ever be to please God, since at the last we must 'appear before the judgement seat of Christ' (v. 10). Since Christ is Saviour and Lord we are responsible to Him. He is our pattern, He is our power. Our measure of conformity to His pattern, and our measure of appropriation of His power, must be judged by Him. It is His judgement seat.

2 CORINTHIANS 5. 11–15

Our Debt to Christ

In the previous study we were reminded of our responsibility to the Lord, and that at His judgement seat we shall have to answer to Him for our behaviour here on earth. Patently we are debtors to Christ. As we have received from Him so we must live our lives for Him. We must ever live with the thought of moral accountancy in mind. Not only must we live with a consciousness of our own responsibility towards God, we must remember that we are responsible for others. This is the lesson Paul teaches in verses 12, 13. This lesson is enforced by certain facts:

1. THE UNIVERSAL IMPLICATIONS OF CHRIST'S DEATH v. 14

'One died for all.' We cannot over emphasise the fact of Christ's death and its implications. It is a case of 'He for us and we for Him', that is, 'one for all and all for one'. All mankind is one in its sin. Observe what this means:

(a) *Sin results in death.* The soul that sins dies. This has been so since the Fall of man. It is the message of the Paradise story. It has been demonstrated repeatedly in the history of mankind. The sinner is dead in trespasses and sins. Being dead he is unable to respond to God. Before there can be response there must be resurrection.

(b) *Death is universal.* 'All were dead.' No human Saviour could have imparted life. If there was to be resurrection, then it had to come from outwith humanity. From time to time in history men have claimed themselves to be the saviours of their fellows, even mankind as a whole. There have been saviours with the sword, saviours with the pen, but none have been able to give resurrection life to a dead humanity.

(c) *Only One could deal with sin and its sequel.* From what we have seen in (a) it is obvious that One who could offer resurrection life was needed above all else. This is precisely what Christ offers, His resurrection life, which is imparted to us by the Holy Spirit. From (b) it is obvious that a Saviour outwith humanity and yet sharing humanity, was required, in other words a Saviour who is Divine. Christ came from heaven not with a sword or a pen but with a cross to die, and then to rise. 'There is none other name under heaven given among men, whereby we must be saved' (Acts 4.12).

2. THE INNER COMPULSION OF CHRIST'S LOVE v. 14

The phrase 'the love of Christ constraineth us' is usually interpreted to mean, our love to Christ compels us to live as Christ would have us do. This however is not what Paul meant. Notice three things:

(a) *The love of Christ is Divine love.* The word *agape*, which means Divine love is employed. Certainly the verb *agapao* is used by Paul to express our love to God, but never the noun, which is used here. Our love for others springs not from human compassion but from Divine concern. It is the expression of the Divine nature which resides within us.

(*b*) *This love is demonstrated in our Lord's own life and death.* How brightly the love of Christ for men shines out in His earthly ministry. He had compassion on those who were hungry, not merely because they had no bread, but because they were 'as sheep without a shepherd' (Mark 6.34). The Fourth Gospel particularly emphasises the love of Christ (John 13.1). Most of all, Christ's love is seen in the cross. This is the extent to which love goes (John 15.13).

(*c*) *This love is shed abroad in our hearts by the Holy Spirit.* It is because of divine love within us that we seek to 'persuade men' (v. 11), so that they may give an account of themselves at the judgement seat of Christ. It is because God hates sin, He judges it, in us; it is because He loves us He provides a means of salvation for us. Because of His love within us we must seek to win others for Him.

3. *THE INESCAPABLE DEMANDS OF CHRIST'S RESURRECTION* v. 15

All that we are and ever hope to be, we owe to Christ. He died that we might live, but we cannot receive His risen life merely to gratify our own desires. His risen life is imparted to us that we might live for His glory. The whole of life now is 'unto Him'.

2 CORINTHIANS 5. 16–21

The New Creation

The previous study introduced us to the new life, which we must now live in Christ. The theme is continued in these verses. We saw in our consideration of verses 6–10 that Paul probably regretted he was not one of the original disciple band, and did not enjoy our Lord's fellowship in the days of His flesh. However he was glad that at the Damascus turnpike he had seen the risen Lord. The church was not so much concerned now with the historic events of His ministry as with the witness of His risen life (v. 16). From 'henceforth' we are not concerned with the externals of any man, but rather the power of the risen Christ which resides within him. What does this mean in effect? It means that the redeemed man has been created anew. He is, to translate literally, 'a new creation'. It is this we must think about as we consider these verses.

1. *THE WONDER OF THE NEW CREATION* v. 17

The Genesis story is repeated in the spiritual realm. Creation was the fiat of God's word, an amazing phenomenon. The new creation is as amazing as the old. Notice three features of this new creation.

(*a*) *It is universal in its appeal.* 'If any man.' Even if we are not ultra Calvinistic in our theology, so often we tend to write off the worst of humanity as unlikely to be redeemed, and perhaps at the back of our minds we secretly believe they are irredeemable. We are more concerned with those on the fringe of the church, who can be won without a great deal of effort. Let us never forget that the offer of God's grace is to 'any man'.

(*b*) *It is total in its scope.* 'He is a NEW creation.' The Christian is not a piece of patched up humanity. He is not someone who is a little better than his fellows, because God has supplied for him the righteousness he lacks. He is not 'a remould' (to use the language of the tyre world), but a new creature. Like Saul of old, God has given him 'another heart' (1 Sam. 10.9). Ezekiel's prophecy is fulfilled (Ezek. 36.26).

(*c*) *It is radical in its implications.* 'Old things are passed away . . . all things are become new.' Every value is changed. There is a completely new scale of values. What was once despised is now loved, what was once cherished is no longer held dear as once it was.

2. THE SECRET OF THE NEW CREATION v. 18

Inevitably men will ask, 'How can this be brought about?' Paul provides the answer.

(a) *It is 'of God'*. Like the creation of the universe, the re-creation of the Christian is not possible apart from Divine power. The message of Genesis 1, is not scientific but religious, namely, that God is the creative power behind the universe in which we live. This is the message here, our new creation is 'of God'. We cannot become new creatures by our own effort, it only becomes possible when we turn to God.

(b) *It is 'by Jesus Christ'*. The prologue of John's gospel tells us that the Word was the agent in creation. 'All things were made by Him and without Him was not anything made that was made' (John 1.3). We must turn to God and look to Christ, if we are to be new creatures, since the new creation is 'by Christ' and 'in Christ'.

(c) *It is through reconciliation*. Paul is careful to make it clear that it is not God who is reconciled to man, but man who is reconciled to God, God taking the initiative and bringing man to Himself.

3. THE MESSAGE OF THE NEW CREATION

This must be passed on. The word is committed to us (v. 19), who have ourselves been reconciled. God has not committed the word of reconciliation to angels, but to redeemed men. Who is more able to speak than the man who from his experience knows that 'God was in Christ reconciling the world unto Himself'? We cannot close this study without emphasising the word 'ambassadors'. We are God's representatives seeking to bring men to the point where they can be reconciled to God and so be at peace with Him. We are however but the bearers of the message. We have no power to reconcile ourselves, this has been done by Christ, who though sinless, was made sin for us. We who had no righteousness of our own, which we could present to God are dependent upon the righteousness God has provided for us in Christ.

Workers Together

The apostle continues the theme of our responsibility in spreading the message of reconciliation. It is God through Christ who provides our salvation, but it is our privilege to proclaim it. In this respect the spread of the kingdom of God is a co-operative effort between God and man. He provides the message, we are His messengers, as 'workers together with Him'. It is an encouraging thought, yet at the same, time as Paul points out here, it is challenging too. If we are to be effective workers, then there are certain caveats we must heed.

1. *WE MUST NOT RECEIVE THE GRACE OF GOD IN VAIN* vv. 1, 2

We are all recipients of God's grace, but if it is to do all that God would have it accomplish in our lives, then it must be accompanied by faith and obedience. The character of God's grace is made clear in verse 2. Notice what grace means,

(*a*) *God hears us when we cry to Him.* The quotation here is from Isaiah 49.8, one of the Servant songs, in which God replies to His servant. We must remember that we are God's servants in that we are workers together with Him. The Master's ear is ever open to the servant. This is grace surely, that we, unworthy as we are, can call upon God and receive an answer.

(*b*) *God succours us in our time of need.* We can all look back across the years and recall how God has wonderfully and graciously intervened on our behalf, when we least deserved His intervention.

(*c*) *God expects us to respond to Him while there is an opportunity to work for him.* Time is a limited commodity, God's day of grace is passing. How vital it is for us to 'redeem the time'! If we waste the precious moments then we are surely receiving God's grace in vain.

2. *WE MUST NOT ALLOW HIS WORK TO SUFFER, BECAUSE OF OUR CONDUCT*
vv. 3–6

The word translated 'approving' in verse 4 really means 'commending'. The question inevitably arises, 'How is this to be done?' There is both a negative and a positive aspect.

(*a*) *Negatively it means 'giving no offence in anything'*. 'No occasion of stumbling' brings out the real sense of the apostle's words. The cross was an offence to the Jew. He could not entertain the idea of a crucified Messiah. He rated the cross so low, he stumbled over it in his pride. It is tragically easy for us to be stumbling blocks, when we are meant to be stepping stones. How terrible it is to cause any of God's children to stumble!

(*b*) *Positively it means a display of Christian virtue*. There must be patience in the midst of outward hardships (vv. 4–5), by which Paul could mean sickness, sorrow, loneliness or perplexity (vide Acts 9.16; 2 Cor. 1.6; 12.7; 2 Tim. 4.10). It would seem from Paul's list, he had in mind the increasing pressures of life which shut us in.

There must also be purity of character, a display of inward graces (v. 6). There must be good intentions motivating our actions. There must be a knowledge of God's will and ways, and also longsuffering and kindness.

3. *WE MUST NOT FAIL TO EMPLOY THE WEAPONS GOD HAS PROVIDED FOR US*
vv. 6, 7

Paul names four in this and the previous verse.

(*a*) *The Holy Ghost*. We can do nothing for God apart from the Holy Spirit. This is something we are so liable to forget, with the result that we act in the energy of the flesh.

(*b*) *Sincere love*, which is the first fruit of the Spirit. If we act without love, then all is in vain (see 1 Cor. 13).

(*c*) *The word of truth*. The Word is a sharp two edged sword. We can say of it as David said of Goliath's sword, 'There is none like it, give it me'.

(*d*) *Divine power*. The gospel is this (Rom. 1.16). If we go to men with any other message we go without the power of God.

(*e*) *The armour of righteousness* (Eph. 6.11 ff.). We need armour that is both defensive and offensive. If we are so clothed then we can be effective workers together with God.

2 CORINTHIANS 6. 8–17

Living for Christ in an Evil Environment

It was certainly not easy to live for Christ in the Roman world, indeed it never has been and never will until the kingdom of Christ comes on earth. Paul unobtrusively moves from the theme of Christian work to that of Christian witness. Our work and our witness go together, indeed our work is really to witness. If we are to live worthily for Christ in our environment, whatever it might be, we must cultivate Christian character, look on the needs of others with compassion and always act with conviction. Character, compassion and conviction are the topics the apostle deals with here.

1. We must notice *THE PARADOX OF CHRISTIAN CHARACTER* vv. 8–10

Paul was much misrepresented by his enemies. It was something that hurt him deeply (vide 1 Cor. 4.12). 'Sticks and stones can break our bones', Paul knew this only too well, but he learnt also that words can wound. How painful a wound can be!

Our Lord was misrepresented. Some said He had a devil. His deeds of love and kindness were attributed to the wrong motives. This was His heartbreak, namely that He came into the world, and unto His own, but His own, did not receive Him. It is little wonder He wept over Jerusalem, knowing as He did what the city was about to do to their Messiah.

The early Christians were misrepresented. They were referred to as 'haters of mankind', as cannibals because the significance of the Lord's supper was not understood by the pagan populace. They

118

were stigmatised as immoral, since they met together to worship in secret. They were accused of being traitors because they acknowledged Jesus as King. So it has been down through history. Wyclif was denounced as a heretic, Wesley was called a 'tub thumper', his followers were denounced as 'Enthusiasts' because they preached the gospel with zeal. The world has never understood the real character of Christianity, and never will until Christ comes again. We must expect to be misrepresented. We may be 'unknown' to the world, but 'known' to God, 'dying' yet gloriously alive to the things of God. 'Sorrowful' in the eyes of men yet rejoicing in the experience of our salvation. 'Poor' as far as earth's possessions are concerned, yet rich in the riches of God's grace.

2. We must display *THE PROOF OF CHRISTIAN COMPASSION* vv. 11–13

Paul's accusers in Corinth had maintained that he had little room for them in his heart. He did not love them. In effect they said he was a loveless and narrow minded man. Far from it, he rejoined that his frankness was not to be misinterpreted as a sign of lovelessness. He had spoken frankly because of his love for them. How true this is! Those who love us most are those who are the most frank with us and correct us when we are wrong. A father corrects and chastises his children because he loves them so much. Alas, we are so often guilty of being 'mealy mouthed' so as not to offend. If we loved sinful men as we claim, then we should be much more forthright with them. How forthright was Jesus, yet never man loved as He loved. The heart which takes in everyone is the heart ready to be frank with those it loves.

3. We must remember *THE PRICE OF CHRISTIAN CONVICTION* vv. 14–17a

It is thought by some scholars that 6.14–7.1 are parenthetical, an interpolation from some other Pauline epistle or not by Paul at all. Certainly they interrupt the appeal he is making; 7.2 follows on naturally from 6.13. However, they contain some very pertinent truths. The Christian must stand out in contrast to the world around. We cannot opt out of society, God does not intend us to do that, but He does intend us to remember that while we are in the world, we do not live by the values of the world. There are some striking contrasts here to emphasise this point. Light is opposed to darkness (v. 14), righteousness with unrighteousness (v. 14), Christ with Belial (v. 15), God with idols (v. 16).

Morally the world has not changed, the unequal yoke is still a danger with which the Christian is faced. Particularly is this so in marriage, and even in business partnerships where the Christian is free to choose his connections.

2 CORINTHIANS 6.17b–7.1

Perfecting Holiness

There is a marked change in verse 17, from precept to promise. This is why it is permissible to divide the verse as we have done. The promises have been freely taken from Isaiah 52.12. It is significant that the Divine blessings promised to Israel are assured to Christians, if they are ready and willing to realise their distinctive place in society. Israel was meant to be a distinctive nation for God, among the peoples of the earth. The Divine intention was that they should be a holy people. Israel had failed God. They had become corrupted by adopting the manners and morals of their neighbours. God's call to us is to be holy. We shall never make an impact on society if we are not 'perfecting holiness in the fear of God'. If this is to be so, then there are three things we must notice.

1. THE MANNER OF LIFE WE MUST LIVE

The Christian's life must be characterised both negatively and positively. Unfortunately far too often it is the negative aspect which has been emphasised at the expense of the positive. Indeed, sometimes the positive aspect is forgotten altogether. However, there is a negative aspect and we must not lose sight of it in our endeavour to be positive. There are things from which we must refrain if our lives are to be pleasing to God.

(*a*) *We must refrain from sins of the flesh* (7.1). Pagan society was characterised by immorality and licentiousness in Paul's day. Pagan worship was often no more than sanctified lust. In our own day there is a decided lowering of moral standards. The cinema, television and the radio, as well as popular literature, is often suggestive, to say the least, and often is almost pornographic. Even the every day conversation is smutty. We live in an age obsessed by sex. The sins of the flesh are tragically easy to commit, when we are bombarded with the lust of the flesh on all sides.

Our affluent society encourages sloth, gluttony and complacency. Let us not forget that these are as much sins of the flesh as sexual indiscretions.

(*b*) *We must refrain from sins of the spirit* (7.1). It is not merely necessary for a Christian to live a moral life, he must search his motives and examine his spirit. The motives that control must ever be the object of our care. It is possible to do God's work for our glory rather than for His.

There is the positive aspect too, referred to here as 'perfecting holiness'. Separation from evil is separation unto God. We can be like the house of which our Lord spoke, swept clean of a demon, but left unoccupied, so that more and worse demons were able to take possession of it. If we think only of that from which we must refrain, then our lives will be terribly negative. If we remind ourselves that we are to refrain from evil in order that we might be sanctified vessels unto God, then life will be gloriously positive for us.

2. THE MOTIVE BY WHICH WE MUST BE INSPIRED

Two motives are suggested to us here. Again there is a positive and a negative emphasis. Let us this time consider the positive first, since it is placed first in the text.

(*a*) *We must be impelled by promises*. There are two 'I wills'. There is the promise of Divine acceptance, 'I will receive you'. God cannot receive us as He would, if we have not taken our stand with Him. It is necessary to 'come out to Him' from the evil world if we expect to be accepted by Him. There is the promise of paternal care, 'and will be a Father unto you'. This was a truth Israel never really appreciated (vide Exod. 4.22; Jer. 31.9; Hos. 1.10), but Jesus has taught us to say 'our Father', and it is through Him we are brought into the family of God.

(b) *We must be restrained by the fear of God.* Notice how the positive of our first heading, is linked with the negative of the second: 'perfecting holiness' which is gloriously positive 'in the fear of God'. Here 'fear' means 'awe'. It is an essential element in religion. Such is lacking today in society. This is why there is so much irreligion. The Old Testament prophets called men to a sense of awe. Let us never forget that God may be Saviour, but He is the righteous Judge also.

3. *THE MOOD WHICH MUST RESULT*

One cannot read these words without feeling the call to determined action. We have promises and precepts, indeed we have every reason to live holy lives. We must stress the phrase, 'Let us'. We are not asked to give this our consideration. We are not called upon to talk about it in our discussion groups, we are challenged to live accordingly. 'Let us . . . perfect holiness,' for our good, but most of all for God's glory.

2 CORINTHIANS 7. 2–16

The Revelation of Paul's Heart

These verses contain one of the most moving appeals in the whole of scripture. Here Paul opens his heart to the Corinthians. Paul had written sternly to them, righteousness demanded that he should. His words of warning had not been written to wound but rather to win them. There are times when all of us have to speak sternly. The tongue and the pen are formidable weapons. We may use them to warn, but never must we use them to wound, rather let the purpose behind our warning be to win. There are four things we can share with Paul, when we are called upon to rebuke someone or something that is wrong.

1. THERE IS A CLAIM WE CAN MAKE v. 2

It is essential that our lives as Christians should be above reproach. If our words of warning are to be effective, at those times when it is necessary for us so to speak, then they must be backed by a life of integrity. If our lives are not characterised by integrity then we had better remain silent. Men like Shaftesbury and Wilberforce were able to speak out against the evils of their day because their lives were without reproach in society. Mark the claim Paul makes with all sincerity.

(a) *He had wronged no man.* No doubt he was referring to the accusations levelled against him, namely that he had lived upon the labours of others (12.14–18), and had misused the authority entrusted to him. We wrong others when we do not treat them as we would be treated ourselves. The employer wrongs his employee when he uses him merely as an economic unit, with no thought of him as a person. The employee wrongs the employer when he does not give the best in his work.

(b) *He had corrupted no man.* This is an even stronger claim to make. We corrupt others when we set a bad example, when we lower our moral standards. We can corrupt too, by the things we say, by suggesting wrong motives, or inciting to greed and lust. We talk of the corrupting influences of the press, advertisements, radio, television and the cinema, but we too can be corrupting agencies.

(c) *He had taken advantage of no man.* This goes even deeper. We can so easily take advantage of the kindness of a neighbour, the skill of a friend which is lacking in us. We can take advantage of the trust that is placed in us. We can take advantage of our loved ones, the faithful devotion of a wife, child, or parent. We are all so guilty of taking things and people for granted. What a challenge Paul's claim presents to us! Yet it is a claim we too can make if our lives are lived as God would have them.

2. THERE IS A COMPASSION WE SHOULD FEEL v. 3

'Ye are in our hearts to die and live with you.' 'In the heart', this is a most intimate phrase. We often tell others that we will 'bear them in mind', meaning that, if we can at some future date do them some kindness then we shall not forget them. Often however it is used as an excuse for escaping from some responsibility, which we are not particularly willing to shoulder. How different to have the interest of someone 'in the heart'.

The phrase 'to die and live with you' does present some difficulty of exposition. Most commentators seem to think that Paul means they will be in his heart both throughout life and as he breathes his last. Yet it may be translated 'to die together and to live together'. It may well be that he is identifying himself with the Corinthian believers, emphasising the fact that they are one in the Lord.

> 'Blest be the tie that binds
> Our hearts in Christian love;
> The fellowship of kindred minds,
> Is like to that above.'

3. THERE IS COMFORT WE CAN ENJOY vv. 4-12

Paul was greatly encouraged to discover from Titus how effective his stern rebuke had been. He was happy to think that frankness had proved to be the best policy. It usually is, even if at first it excites the anger of those who eventually see the folly of their ways (v. 4). Paul was terribly anxious until Titus brought him the happy news from Corinth. We can be comforted and rejoice as Paul did in

(a) *The way in which God works* (v. 6). This epistle is concerned with the comfort of God more than with anything else. Already he had made it clear that God is the God of all comfort. Again he emphasises that it is God who brings comfort. Notice that God brings comfort through others. In this case it was Titus. It is a comfort to have one's friends and loved ones in times of sorrow.

(b) *Godly sorrow results in life* (v. 10). There is 'sorrow' and 'sorrow'. It is one thing to be sorry for ourselves, quite another to be sorry for our sins. Self pity gets us nowhere, but repentance brings us into life. The evidence of life is to be found expressed so emphatically in verse 11. Mark the words he uses, 'carefulness', 'clearing', 'indignation', 'desire', 'zeal', and 'revenge'.

4. *THERE IS A CONFIDENCE WE MAY HAVE*
vv. 13–16

The repentance of the Corinthians showed the kind of Christians they were. Paul's love had always thought the best of them and he had boasted of them to Titus. He could boast now even more. Frankness leads to faith. If we are frank with others, they know they can trust us, and if our frankness leads to their repentance, then we know we can trust them. The world and the church is crying out for mutual trust.

2 CORINTHIANS 8. 1–6

The Proof of God's Grace

In these verses Paul presents the Macedonian churches as an example to the Corinthian believers. Corinth was a flourishing city, and it seems that the church in Corinth shared the opulence of the city. Gaius, with whom Paul stayed when he was writing his Roman epistle, is generally thought to have been a wealthy man. Corinth presented a striking contrast to the rest of Greece. Macedonia was particularly poor. Churches such as those at Philippi, Thessalonica and Beroea probably had little of this world's goods. In our affluence we must never forget the poverty of others. We must mark the most commendable conduct of the Macedonian believers. We notice three things concerning them.

1. *THE PARADOX OF THEIR POSITION*

We can never judge a church by its outward appearance. Alas, we so often do. We are impressed with its magnificence, and its

125

adornments, when what really counts is the calibre of its membership, the impact that it is making on the community in which it is situated, and its witness throughout the world, through its missionary interest. (Contrast the church in Smyrna [Rev. 2.8–11] with that in Laodicea [Rev. 3.14–22], particularly 2.9 with 3.17.) Let us examine the paradox of the Macedonian witness.

(a) *Though they were tried yet they were joyful* (v. 2). Notice the words employed, 'great' trial, that is, most severe affliction, but 'abundance' of joy. Like the early apostles they rejoiced that they were privileged to suffer for Christ. We do not usually associate affliction and joy, but we can do so in Christian witness and experience.

(b) *Though they were poor yet they gave liberally* (v. 2). The word translated 'deep' means literally 'deep down'. It stands in contrast to abounding riches of their liberality. Their giving was comparable to that of the widow who gave her mites. How often those who have least to give, give most!

(c) *Though they were apparently powerless to help yet they gave beyond such power as they had* (v. 3). How striking the paradox is presented to us here! Powerless, yet Paul writes 'according to their power', and then adds, 'yea, beyond their power'. It is sometimes said that 'you cannot get blood out of a stone'. The liberality of the Macedonian Christians in the midst of their poverty gives the lie to that.

2. THE PASSION OF THEIR PERSUASION v. 4

It appears that Paul was thinking of exempting them from giving towards the needs of the poor saints in Jerusalem, but they were determined to play their part. Literally verses 3 and 4 read 'of their own accord begging of us with much entreaty'. Here in these words we learn the manner in which we should give.

(a) *Willingly.* 'Were willing of themselves' or 'of their own accord'. They did not have to be asked. They had heard of the needs of the saints in Jerusalem, and no doubt felt for them because they were experiencing poverty themselves. So often we do not give until we are asked. If we were willing to give, then we would be well aware of some need or other, and give to relieve it without being asked to do so.

(b) *Earnestly*. As one commentator remarks, 'This is something beyond mere spontaneity in giving'. They implored the apostle that they might be allowed to give. They did not rejoice that Paul knew of their poverty and was not asking them to commit themselves, rather, they were sorry that the apostle had seen fit to exempt them. They had two obstacles to overcome, firstly, that of finding something to give in their poverty, and secondly, having made their offering, persuading Paul to accept it.

(c) *Co-operatively*. Paul uses the phrase 'the fellowship of the ministering'. When we give we have fellowship in the ministry of the Word. We may not be able to preach ourselves or go to the mission field, but by our giving we are enabling others to go and preach. We are co-operating in the work of the Lord.

3. *THE POWER OF THEIR PRODIGALITY*

Why was it they were able to give, when so poor? The answer is here: 'they gave themselves to the Lord'. Their sense of stewardship stemmed from this. Stewardship campaigns are bound to fail if there is not first and foremost surrender to the Lord on the part of His people. Corinth could not have had a better example than that of their poor brethren in Macedonia. Though poor yet they were abundantly rich.

The Grace of Giving

Having presented the example of the Macedonian Christians to the church in Corinth, Paul now exhorts them to give in the same spirit. The Macedonians gave out of their poverty, Paul exhorts the Corinthians to give out of their plenty (v. 7). He makes it clear in verse 8 that this must not be interpreted as an apostolic command. He did not want anything from them that was unwillingly given. There would be no grace in such giving. That which is given grudgingly is better not given at all. He rejoiced over the news of their repentance brought to him by Titus (v. 6). He felt that a freewill offering from them would prove the sincerity of their protestations of repentance. Grace in giving is something which must be expressed by us.

1. IT IS DEMANDED BY THE NEED FOR A BALANCED CHRISTIAN LIFE

The Corinthian church gloried in its gifts. Paul recognised this as a fact, 'Ye abound in everthing,' he wrote, and then went on to name some of the gifts they possessed. There was no lack of 'faith' in Corinth. In 1 Cor. 12.9 it is mentioned as one of the gifts of the Spirit. Indeed we cannot enjoy faith apart from the work of the Spirit. He names 'utterance' as another gift. It may be he was referring to the gift of tongues, or he may have had in mind their ability to preach the gospel. A further grace is 'knowledge'. They were spiritually intelligent people in Corinth, diligent and loving too. Patently their hearts and their lips were dedicated to the Lord, but if they were to be balanced in their Christian life, then the hand needed to be devoted to the Lord as well. The grace of giving is always a practical expression of the faith and love we profess, and the gospel we proclaim. Giving liberally would prove the sincerity of their love (v. 8).

2. IT IS DEMANDED BY THE EXAMPLE OF OUR LORD

They knew much about the grace of the Lord Jesus in Corinth. Paul informs them that grace is giving. Grace has been defined as 'unmerited love', and love delights to give as we know from John 3.16. This is so beautifully expressed here.

(a) *Grace empties itself.* It pours itself out in lavish abundance. 'Though he was rich, yet for your sakes he became poor.' We have only to think of the wonder of the incarnation, and what it must have meant for the Son of God, to understand this. We can read Philippians chapter 2 in conjunction with this, since it is a commentary on the marvel of God's grace in Christ.

128

(b) *Grace is concerned with others.* 'For your sakes.' Christ came to 'seek and to save that which was lost'. The whole of Christ's ministry was concerned with others. On the Cross He prayed for those who crucified Him, and commended His mother to the apostle who stood with her.

(c) *Grace is poured out that it might be poured into us.* 'That ye through his poverty might be rich.' It has most certainly been poured out for us, but the question we must ask ourselves is 'Have we received it as we should?' Poured out, but has it been poured into us? He became poor, but was it in vain as far as we are concerned? Are we living on the riches of His grace?

3. *IT IS DEMANDED BY THE NEED OF OTHERS* v. 14

Evidently the Corinthians had already initiated a collection (v. 10), but those things which had troubled the church held up the work of collecting. Now he appeals to them to continue and complete the task, not only because of the need there was in Jerusalem, but also that there might be a bond of fellowship between the two churches. Giving leads to mutual responsibility. If they in Corinth gave according to their ability to the saints in Jerusalem, then at some future date, if there was need in Corinth, the saints in Jerusalem could not possibly ignore it. By giving one to another we are indebted to one another. The bonds of fellowship are strengthened.

2 CORINTHIANS 8. 16–24

God's Messengers

Paul sent Titus and two other brethren to Corinth to receive the offering. The identity of the brethren who accompanied Titus is not disclosed, yet they are highly commended. In the religious world there are those who hit the headlines, their names will go down in history as leaders and evangelists of the age, but there are countless others who labour unknown, yet known to God and highly commended by His people. These two brethren sent by Paul remind us of the vast army of the unknown who labour for the Lord. They are God's messengers, commended by Him. We can learn much from these verses about God's messengers. Let us notice:

1. THE QUALITIES WHICH SHOULD CHARACTERISE GOD'S MESSENGERS

What is it that commends a messenger, both to God and to those among whom he labours? The qualities which are essential to any messenger are portrayed by Titus and his brethren.

(a) *Concern* (v. 16). Paul describes it as 'care in the heart'. If we are to be God's messengers then we should at all times be concerned for the welfare of others. It is tragically easy for the messenger to be concerned for his own prestige and reputation. It has been said that the secret of J.O.Y. is 'Jesus first', 'Others next' and 'Yourself last'. How true this is!

(b) *A reputation as a preacher of the gospel* (v. 18). 'Whose praise is in the gospel,' that is, who is known for his proclamation of the gospel. A messenger must be known by his message, not because of what he is in himself, that is not important. The message is all important. There is no greater honour than to be called 'a preacher of the gospel'.

(c) *Diligence* (v. 22), or 'Earnestness'. An alternative rendering says, 'our brother, whom we have many times proved earnest in many things'. Paul gives a further reason for his diligence, namely, confidence in the Corinthian believers. The A.V. suggests that the confidence is Paul's, but this is by no means clear in the Greek. It may possibly be the confidence of the messenger, which seems more logical. Diligence and earnestness must accompany the Lord's work. We must never approach it apathetically and lethargically, but always earnestly.

2. THE INCENTIVES WHICH SHOULD IMPEL GOD'S MESSENGERS

Inevitably the question arises, 'Why should God's messengers display these qualities above all others?' The answer is to be found in this passage.

(a) *Because they are the bearers of gifts.* By 'this grace' (v. 19), Paul means 'this gift for the saints in Judaea'. They bore love from one church to another. This is our privilege, we must never abuse it. It is so easy to carry evil reports and gossip from one to another. How much better to strengthen the bonds of fellowship by carrying love! Not only did they bring 'this particular gift' or 'grace', they bore also as we do, the 'gift of God' or 'grace of God'. Our privilege is to proclaim the message of God's grace by presenting God's gift to men.

(b) *Because they lived solely for God's glory* (vv. 19, 23). Twice the word 'glory' appears on the written page, but it should ever be in the forefront of our minds. We bring the offer of salvation, and proclaim the gospel, not primarily even for the salvation of men, but with a view to God's glory.

(c) *Because they are channels ever ready for the Lord to use* (v. 19). This is the meaning of the latter part of this verse. The A.V. indicates that the readiness is that of the Corinthians, but many scholars feel that 'our' is a preferable translation to 'your'. However we may wish to translate this phrase, it is clear that the 'grace' is administered by us, that is, we are channels of grace. The thought of this should send us out rejoicing in the privilege which is ours through Christ.

3. THE MANNER IN WHICH WE SHOULD CONDUCT OURSELVES AS GOD'S MESSENGERS vv. 20–21

The phrase used in verse 20, 'avoiding this', is a nautical one. It can be used to denote shifting sail, to avoid the enemy in battle. Paul means we should not act so as to bring us into conflict with anyone. We should always behave so as to avoid criticism. Of course, he is here primarily referring to the offering which was to be taken from the Corinthians. He was eager to avoid any criticism of mismanagement. The operative word in verse 21 is surely 'honest'. The messenger must always be open, so as never to be afraid of the scrutiny of men or of God.

2 CORINTHIANS 9. 1–7

Be Prepared

It is obvious from these verses that Paul was not overconfident about the Corinthian church, in spite of the fact that in the previous year they had initiated the offering. After the disturbances which had occurred, the apostle felt that asking them for money was a very delicate matter. He writes most courteously to them, with amazing tactfulness. He was not sure how they would react. If he dropped the matter, and they heard that others had given while they had not, no doubt Paul feared that they would be offended. The Christian finds himself in many such a difficult situation. We need great grace in dealing with others. Notice that Paul not only deals with the matter tactfully, but characteristically he draws spiritual lessons from the situation. There are several lessons we can learn from this passage.

1. OUR ZEAL CAN BE AN INCENTIVE TO OTHERS v. 2

He had commended the liberality of the Macedonians. This could easily be misinterpreted by the church in Corinth. If Macedonia had displayed generosity in giving, then Corinth was characterised by zeal. The fact they had initiated the offering was probably responsible for the liberality of others. The word 'zeal' is most suggestive. It is from this word that the Zealots took their name. They were the revolutionaries of the age.

(a) *Zeal is something which involves self sacrifice.* The Zealot was ready to take any risk in the cause of patriotism. The man who is zealous in some cause or other, is ready to sacrifice time and money

132

to further his cause. Zeal should characterise our service for the Master.

(b) *Zeal is like a fire that spreads.* It provokes interest in others, so that eventually they too become zealous. Alas, so often we are far more zealous to enlist the support of men for other causes than that of Christ. Our lives are without fire. If we are not on fire for God ourselves, we shall never kindle a blaze in the hearts of others.

(c) *Zeal is a personal quality.* Literally this reads, 'Zeal from you'. We must never forget that the church is the integration of its members. A church will not be zealous if its members are not so. Mark the personal pronoun 'you'. Let us ask ourselves, 'Am I as zealous as I should be?' It is a personal question which must be answered by us individually.

2. OUR UNPREPAREDNESS CAN BE AN EMBARRASSMENT TO OTHERS

Zeal is a most commendable quality, but it has to be disciplined and marshalled into the right channels. Even guerilla warfare has to be organised if it is to be effective. The zealous man may ever be campaigning yet never bring his campaigns to a successful conclusion. He can be so engrossed in what he is doing, that he is unprepared when the call to action comes. This was Paul's fear concerning the Corinthians. It is so easy to talk and never to do. It takes nothing to say 'Amen'; it involves an act of will to see that what we desire is achieved.

> 'Give me the will to fashion as I feel. . . .
> Knowledge I ask not, knowledge thou has lent,
> But, Lord, the will, there lies my deepest need.'
> *John Drinkwater*

When our call comes to act let us see that we are prepared for action, and that we are neither an embarrassment to others nor to God.

3. OUR GIVING CAN BE A HELP TO OTHERS

Giving involves both principle and practice.

(a) *The principle is to be found in verse 6.* The farmer who does

133

not sow plentifully cannot expect so to reap. We only receive in proportion to our giving. The farmer sows his seed that he may sell his produce. He does not sow merely for his own needs. He sows to meet the needs of others. We cannot expect to meet the needs of others if we do not give ourselves wholeheartedly, that is, zealously (see 1 above). If the farmer does not sow as he should, famine will result. When challenged by the need of others he will be unprepared to meet it (see 2 above).

(b) *The practice of giving is to be found in verse 7.*

   i. *It is to be the result of thought and deliberation.* 'As he purposeth in his heart.' Not something that is done haphazardly.

   ii. *It is to be as liberal as it can possibly be.* 'Not grudgingly', or in a niggardly manner. Not the least we can get away with, but the most we can afford.

   iii. *It is to be a willing offering.* 'Not of necessity,' that is, not because we cannot avoid giving, but because we delight in giving. Our delight is shared by God, for 'God loveth a cheerful giver'.

2 CORINTHIANS 9. 8–15

God's Sufficiency

In these verses Paul makes it clear that we can give because all the resources of the universe are at God's disposal. We can give to others because we can draw upon these resources. Indeed, we have nothing of our own. All that we have comes from Him, and is to be used for His glory in meeting the needs of others. Here Paul points out that this is a Divine triangle of blessing. Everything is derived from God, He is the apex of the triangle. Blessing flows to us at one point, in order that it might be passed on to others at the third point. From this point arises thanksgiving to God, which brings us back to the apex from where we begin, and from where all is derived. What does this teach us? Surely three things.

1. GOD IS ABLE TO PROVIDE

In everything we must begin with God. This is so at the commencement of our natural life. This is so too with our spiritual life. It is so also in the process of blessing. The passage begins with the words, 'And (or, 'for') God. . . .' The 'He' of verse 9 is God. When God supplies, He does so abundantly. We must not fail to notice the 'alls' in this passage. Mark that God's provision is

(a) *All grace.* By this Paul means every gift, no matter what its nature, material or spiritual. Grace as we have seen is unmerited love. We deserve absolutely nothing, but God not merely gives us the necessities of life, He makes these gifts abound. Corinth boasted of its spiritual gifts. It may be there was a danger that the Corinthians felt these gifts were the result of their own abilities. Paul tactfully reminds them they are from God.

(b) *Always.* So often the Christian feels that he is spiritually poor; he bewails his low spiritual state. There is no excuse for this. God's gifts are not merely abundant in special seasons of spiritual blessing, during an evangelistic campaign or at some special convention, but all the time.

(c) *All sufficient.* This needs to be emphasised. We may rejoice in the wide variety of gift, which is ours at all times, but we can rejoice too that the gift will always be adequate to the situation in which we find ourselves. We have already seen in our study of this epistle that we can always be triumphant over circumstances. This is because of the all sufficiency of gift which is ours.

(d) *For all purposes.* This is what Paul means by 'every good work'. We have been brought into fellowship with God, through Christ, that we may work for Him. His work is good, and He supplies the grace that these good works may be performed by us. Not only is there all sufficiency for every situation, there is all sufficiency for every task. No matter what the task to which we are called, we can be sure He will supply the gift to do it.

2. WE ARE ABLE TO PRAISE vv. 11–13

'Being enriched' results in 'thanksgiving to God'. This is repeated in verse 12 and in verse 13 we read 'they glorify God'. The praise flows from the provision. That is why the phrase 'being enriched' is so important, it sums up what Paul has been writing. We can inquire again as to the nature of this enrichment and our cause for praise. We discover that we have reason for praise in that

(*a*) *God has moved men to dispense His bounty* (v. 9). The quotation is from Psalm 112.9. How good it is that there have been those who have sown the seed of God's Word, and ministered to those in need! We can rejoice that down through the ages, there have been those who have made it their business to extend God's kingdom. We are part of it because of their faithfulness. Let us thank God for the human agencies He employs.

(*b*) *Our sowing of seed bears fruit in other lives.* The seed being sown not only meets our need by bearing fruit in us, but this same seed in our hand can 'increase the fruits of your righteousness' (v. 10), that is, can make it possible for us to be greater channels of blessing. The word 'righteousness' here means beneficence; Paul is not using it in a theological sense as in Romans.

(*c*) *The needs of the saints are met.* Verse 12 literally reads, 'filling up the wants of the saints'. There are empty stomachs which need food, there are ignorant minds which need instruction, there are hungry souls which need nourishment. Happily the saints can be filled with the wisdom of God.

3. *OTHERS ARE ABLE TO PRAY* v. 14

Since God provides, we praise God for His provision in ministering to the wants of others. Those whom we serve in the gospel pray for us. It is a comfort to know that those to whom we minister pray for us. It is by prayer we are supported in our work. We may minister to others in the gospel, but others minister to us in prayer. So the work of God goes forward. We depend upon one another, but all depend upon Him.

Dealing with the Difficult Situation

Patently Paul sounds a very different note here, and indeed throughout the remainder of the epistle. Many scholars consequently believe that in these closing chapters we have part of another epistle which the apostle wrote, before he received the news of the Corinthian believers' repentance. Certainly here, Paul is dealing with a difficult situation. We do well to notice how firm he is, yet how courteous in his approach. We need to be firm where there is wrong. No good ever comes from weakness in such a situation. Nor does any good come through discourtesy. We can be firm yet courteous. In this passage we are reminded of three vital facts concerning our relationship with Christ.

1. *OUR WITNESS TO CHRIST*

How do we react when we have been slandered or misinterpreted as Paul had been? No doubt most of us hurriedly take up arms to defend our reputation. This is quite natural and understandable, but is it always the right way for a Christian to act? How did Christ react to slanderous accusations made against Him? Usually He ignored them, or contented Himself with some comment. He certainly did not hasten to defend Himself at all costs. Before Herod, He never opened His mouth. Paul by his behaviour in this difficult situation witnessed to Christ's indwelling power in his life.

(*a*) *He did so by his entreaty.* He did not order, but entreated. 'I beseech you', he wrote. He believed that good sense could reign in Corinth, and appealed to their good sense. It is tragically possible to win a victory and lose a friend. Paul's heart is in this appeal. Notice the personal note, 'I Paul myself'. Paul was a forceful personality, and he knew when to use the force of his personality in the cause of righteousness and peace.

(*b*) *He did so by his meekness.* Jesus declared in the Beatitudes, 'Blessed are the meek: for they shall inherit the earth' (Matt. 5.5). Meekness is not a quality which gains much respect in our modern world, but wherever it is displayed it is a testimony to Christ. In His gracious invitation (Matt. 11.29) Jesus declared 'I am meek and lowly in heart'. We are never more Christlike than when we are meek.

(c) *He did so by his gentleness*. Again we have one of the outstanding characteristics of the Master. It is true that He could use physical force when it was called for, as in the cleansing of the Temple, but we associate Christ rather with the reprimand addressed to Peter in the garden, when he seized the sword severing the ear of Malchus. We associate the Master with the action of taking the little children into His arms and blessing them.

(d) *He did so by his lowliness*. Literally it reads 'before your face am lowly among you'. His accusers in Corinth declared that when he was absent from them he could write strong letters, but when he was present in Corinth he was too lowly to reprimand them. Paul here declares that he is both lowly in their presence and while absent from them. Yet he is ever courageous to denouce evil. We can be both lowly and courageous.

2. *OUR WARFARE FOR CHRIST* vv. 2–5

We must remember that we have not only to witness to Christ, we have to wage a warfare for Christ. This is what Paul was doing in Corinth. The devil was busy destroying the effective witness of the church, and at all costs he needed to be stopped. Inevitably the question arises, 'How can we defeat the evil one?'

(a) *There must be courage rooted in confidence* (v. 2). Paul was not afraid of his accusers in Corinth. He was prepared to face them, because he knew that his cause was right. We can be bold when we are confident our cause is right.

(b) *There must be power from God* (v. 2). Though we have to wage war against the flesh, we have spiritual weapons which have been provided for us by the armoury of God. The army which has the superior weapons has a decided advantage. So have we.

(c) *There must be correct strategy* (v. 5). An army destroys the centres of enemy power and having destroyed them, takes them over for its own use. This is what we must do. We must bring 'into captivity every thought'. It is a great task, but nothing is impossible with God.

3. OUR WALK WITH CHRIST v. 6

Man's warfare against God is the expression of his disobedience. Man's obedience is expressed in his walk with God. The trouble makers in Corinth were at war not only with Paul but also with God. They were disobedient to the Divine will. Paul longed for their obedience to be fulfilled. God longs that ours is too, so that we may walk in fellowship with Him.

2 CORINTHIANS 10. 7–18

A Right Perception

In these verses, Paul continues his defence against the slanderous accusations made against him, by his detractors in Corinth. Some thought by opposing Paul they were 'calling bluff'. They maintained that the apostle was good at writing strong letters but weak when it came to facing his opponents. Paul affirms that this is not so (v. 11). He denied that he basked in the sunshine of self glory (v. 13). His one concern was to proclaim the gospel of Christ (v. 16). He neither commends himself nor seeks the commendation of others, but desires the Lord's approval (v. 18). This is not an easy passage to understand, but it is a passage which teaches us three important lessons.

1. THE TRAGEDY OF ECCLESIASTICAL EXCLUSIVISM v. 7

The 'Christ' party in Corinth claimed that they exclusively belonged to Christ. Paul did not deny that those who belonged to this party were Christ's but he did object to being excluded from a privilege which was his by virtue of Divine grace. So much of the sectarianism which has so sadly divided the church springs from ecclesiastical exclusivism. It is surely a terrible thing to deny the right of fellowship to one who belongs to Christ. We do well to inquire more carefully into the nature and implications of such exclusivism.

(*a*) *It is a refusal to see the completeness of the church.* Ecclesiastical exclusivism limits the church to one particular ecclesiastical system. It is a failure to 'discern' the body of Christ as an integrated whole. Jesus rebuked his disciples in the days of His flesh when they reported that they saw one casting out devils in His Name, and they forbade him because, as they put it, 'he followeth not us' (Mark 9.38).

(*b*) *It exposes a narrow self confidence.* Mark the phrase 'If any man trust to himself'. Those who act exclusively boast of themselves, they parade their rightness before others. They display the spirit of the Pharisee which our Lord condemned, that is, the spirit of self righteousness, which breeds bigotry.

(*c*) *It displays a neglect of self reflection.* 'Let him of himself think this again', that is, let him reflect on the claim he is making. When we reflect upon what it means to be Christ's, when we forsake the spirit of narrow self confidence, then immediately we see how great is the circle of God's love, and how many it embraces who do not necessarily see eye to eye with us. How right Faber was when he wrote:

> 'For the love of God is broader
> Than the measures of man's mind:
> And the heart of the Eternal
> Is most wonderfully kind'

2. *THE GLORY OF CHRISTIAN MISSION*

Exclusivism is tragically negative. It draws a circle to keep the few in and the multitude out. There is nothing exclusive about the gospel, it is to all. It proclaims that 'Whosoever will may come'. In this passage we discover precisely where this glory rests.

(*a*) *In the fact that the Christian mission involves proclamation.* Verse 14 contains the phrase 'preaching the gospel of Christ'. Certainly the word 'preaching' is not to be found in the original, but it is implied. Paul had come as far west as Corinth preaching the gospel of Christ. This was his primary aim, to proclaim Christ as Saviour and Lord. There is nothing more glorious than this. The thought is repeated in verse 16.

(b) *Christian mission involves edification* (v. 8). It must have seemed to many in Corinth that Paul's severe rebuke was aimed at humbling them to the dust. Paul however makes it clear that it was his intention to 'build up' the believers in Corinth rather than destroy their faith. The gospel is not merely a message of the salvation of men from the penalty of sin, it is the good news that men can be completely delivered from the power of sin. It is not only concerned with initial decision for Christ, but the Christian's walk with Christ. Let us not fail to proclaim the whole counsel of God.

(c) *Christian mission involves anticipation* (v. 15). Notice the phrase 'having hope'. When we sow the seed of the Word, either through the spoken message or the written word, we do so in the hope that it will bring forth fruit. Paul did not despair of the Corinthians. He knew the power of the word and was confident that it would bear fruit in the Corinthian church. Every sower sows in anticipation of the harvest.

3. *THE VALIDITY OF GOD'S CALLING*

Much is said about validity of ecclesiastical ordination. In some circles ordination rests upon church commendation, while in others it rests upon ecclesiastical succession. Paul certainly makes clear that no man can commend himself as a minister of the gospel, but he places the emphasis of ordination where it should be placed, namely, with the Lord. No matter what denominational view we may take, if our ordination is not that of the pierced hands of Christ then it is invalid.

The Care of Christ's Church

In these verses Paul expresses his deep concern over the state of the church in Corinth. From what he had written to them by way of rebuke, and more especially from the manner in which he had written to them, it may have appeared to many in Corinth that the great apostle had lost his love for them. Here he makes it clear that he had written sternly because he loved them deeply. His heart was pained to see the havoc, which both their divisions and spiritual laxity had caused within the fellowship, impairing its witness. Real love is not slow to rebuke, when rebuke is called for. God rebukes us because He loves us, and cannot bear to see the tragedy that sin brings about in human lives.

I. *A JUSTIFICATION FOR DIVINE JEALOUSY*

Paul writes of being 'jealous' and of 'jealousy'. Jealousy to us is something obnoxious. It is a word which has deteriorated in meaning. In scripture when it is used of God, it indicated God's passionate concern. This is the way in which Paul uses it here. Human jealousy is concerned with its own honour and prestige. It grasps its object selfishly. But this is not so with Divine jealousy, although it is true that God will not share our lives with evil. Divine love delights to give and to share. God wants us that he might share us with others. Why is God jealous over us? Why was Paul jealous over the church in Corinth?

(*a*) *Because they were betrothed to Christ, as we are betrothed to Him*. It is a familiar Old Testament figure (Isa. 54.5; 62.5; Hos. 2.19). It is one, also which Paul employed (Eph. 5.23–25). It recurs again in the Revelation, where the church is referred to as the 'Bride', the Lamb's wife (21.9). Betrothal carries with it a demand for faithfulness.

(*b*) *Because their purity of life was involved*. Unfaithfulness brings with it impurity. We are saved from the penalty of sin that we might live lives which are pure. God's purpose for us is that we

142

might enjoy an intimate relationship with Christ. Our relationship to Christ is a challenge to our conduct.

(c) *Because there was a danger that their affections would be alienated from Christ* (v. 3). Henry Drummond wrote of 'the expulsive power of a new affection', in describing Christ's love, but we must remember that other loves may expel the love of Christ from our hearts. Nothing is more tragic than a loveless marriage. Yet how many Christians betrothed to Christ have lost their love for Him.

2. THE PROCLAMATION OF A SPURIOUS MESSAGE

We can hardly miss the repetition of the word 'another' (v. 4). Notice how Paul uses it.

(a) *Another Jesus.* Christ is the foundation of the church, the rock on which it stands. Paul had reminded the Corinthians in his first epistle that there was no other foundation, nor indeed could there be any other foundation. We have only to examine the Christologies of some of the heresies to be found in the early centuries of church history, or for that matter the Christologies of some of the modern cults, to realise that there are other Jesuses than that of the orthodox faith. Our message must ever be judged by the picture it portrays of Christ.

(b) *Another spirit.* John in his first epistle warned his readers that there were many spirits, and called upon them to 'try the spirits whether they are of God' (1 John 4.1). Only when Christ is rightly presented will the Holy Spirit do His work of conviction and conversion. The Holy Spirit is the Spirit of Christ. We cannot expect the Christ who lived and died and rose again to reside in our hearts, apart from the agency of the Holy Spirit.

(c) *Another gospel.* Gospel means good news. The world has repeatedly been presented with panaceas which it has been said would cure its ills. They have been proclaimed as the gospel for the age to which they belong. They are other gospels. The Gospel however is ageless, since it meets the needs of every age and generation. There would be no counterfeit if there were no genuine article. The counterfeit however, is often so like the genuine article we need to have great discernment. How vital it is for us to be so acquainted with the true Gospel that we readily discern that which is spurious and false!

3. THE MANIFESTATION OF A GENUINE CONCERN

There was no doubt as to the character of the gospel Paul proclaimed, since he himself was a product of its power. We have only to consider the apostle's character to realise that here was indeed the embodiment of the good news. We must ever be an advertisement for the gospel we proclaim, the Spirit we experience and the Jesus we have received. Notice Paul's:

(a) *Self-effacing humility* (v. 7). He had abased himself that the Corinthian believers might be exalted. Truly he had written to them with apostolic authority, but authority and humility are not mutually exclusive. We can speak with authority yet speak in humility. Indeed we always must so speak.

(b) *Generous liberality* (v. 8). This may not be obvious from a casual reading of the verse. Paul uses strong language, which of course must be interpreted hyperbolically. His meaning is that he had taken wages of others (the word is that used of a soldier's rations) that he might be no burden to the church in Corinth. In other words, he had given of his service freely. In this he had followed the example of His Master. He, though rich with all the wealth of heaven, experienced the poverty of earth for those who wrong him. This indeed is grace, the unmerited love of God in Christ, and grace above all else, displays the concern of God for men.

2 CORINTHIANS 11. 10–33

Defeating the Evil Purpose of the Enemy

In these verses Paul issues a further warning against false teachers and then goes on to defend his own actions. If he has appeared boastful, it has not been to exalt himself, but rather to meet the accusations made against him by his detractors. They had sought to belittle him, but whatever claim they might make, he could equal it. There was one significant difference between them and him, namely, that they gloried in their strength, he gloried in his weakness (v. 30). Paul was a man who knew that Divine strength could be made perfect in human weakness. This is the lesson of this passage: How we can meet the foe effectively?

1. EVIL DOERS ARE REFUTED BY RIGHT ACTIONS

There is no need for anyone to meet evil with evil. This is the mistake man has made throughout history. Evil acts have been met with yet other evil deeds. Evil can only effectively be overcome by good. We must not miss the emphasis Paul makes here on 'doing' (v. 12).

(*a*) *Men resort to self transformation, but we can rely upon Divine transformation* (v. 13). He quotes the case of Satan himself. He can transform himself into an angel of light when it suits his purpose. It is not surprising therefore if his slaves similarly transform themselves. We need to remember Paul's word in his Roman epistle, 'be ye transformed' (Rom. 12.2). There is a world of difference between self transformation and Divine transformation. One is often no more than reformation, the other is always regeneration.

(*b*) *Men resort to disguise, but we are designed according to God's pattern.* In war, decoys are used to mislead the enemy. Often decoys look like the real thing. Our word hypocrite comes from the Greek word which means an actor, one who pretends to be something he is not. We are not hypocrites, not acting a part, but living a life designed for us by God.

(*c*) *Men reap the fruits of their own labour, but we see the fruit of God's Spirit working in us.* Men's efforts are displays of fleshly energy, our work is the demonstration of the power of God. We do not need to lower ourselves to the level of the enemies of the cross in the tactics we employ. We can be sure that God will effect His purpose by His power in us, and through us in His world.

2. DECEITFUL SERVANTS ARE EXPOSED BY FAITHFUL SERVICE vv. 23-28

Here Paul refers to his racial descent. It seems that much of the opposition to him in Corinth came from those who either were unconverted Jews, or those, who had been converted, but objected to his openness in admitting the Gentiles to the church without subjecting them to Jewish rites. Paul makes it clear that it is not race that really matters, but grace. Though grace is God's un-merited love freely given, it carries with it implications.

(*a*) *We must work for Him.* We are ministers or servants of Christ (v. 23). We can echo the words of the poet when he writes,

> 'I cannot work my soul to save
> For this my Lord hath done;
> But I can work like any slave
> For the love of God's dear Son.'

His grace demands our service. We can do no other than work for Him. We must ever remember that we are His servants, and must be ready to obey His every command.

(*b*) *We must be prepared to suffer with Him* (vv. 23-27). Paul recites many of the perils and privations he has faced and endured. It is unlikely that many of us suffer as Paul suffered, but we can be sure at some stage in life's journey we shall be called upon to face persecution for Him.

(*c*) *We must be prepared to shoulder responsibility for Him* (v. 28). Paul had the care of the churches on his heart and mind. We are our brother's keeper. None of us can live to ourselves if we are living for God. It is a lesson which we are slow to learn. So often we are content to enjoy our own salvation and disregard the needs of others.

3. VAIN BOASTERS ARE SILENCED BY DIVINE METHODS vv. 29-33

Paul was conscious of his human weakness, but through it he experienced Divine strength. That is why he gloried in his infirmities, because it was in them that he experienced most the power of God. The pilgrim who passes through the valley of Baca

146

makes it a well, and he who is troubled in the valley of Achor (trouble) finds it to be a door of hope (Hos. 2.15).

2 CORINTHIANS 12. 1–16

From the Lord

In these verses Paul continues to defend his apostleship. He does so however, in a most unusual way. In the previous chapter he most certainly boasts of the privilege which God had conferred on him, but he makes it plain that apostleship involves hardship. In this chapter one would hardly realise that he is writing of himself, especially as we read the opening verses. Verses 1–4 are undoubtedly difficult to expound. In fact, Paul found it difficult to explain the experience he is describing. We must therefore on no account dogmatise. Many of God's people have had similar experiences to that of Paul, and those who have been denied them, must not gainsay the experience of those who have. There are three lessons we can learn from this passage.

1. *WE MUST ALWAYS GLORY IN OUR SPIRITUAL EXPERIENCE AS FROM THE LORD*

So often those who claim to have enjoyed some extraordinary spiritual experience, are boastful about it for their own glory. The man who has a genuine experience of the Lord in this way will give God the glory. This is what Paul does here. Notice how he does so.

(a) *He makes it clear that his visions and revelations are OF THE LORD.* It is significant to notice they are not visions of the future. They do not claim to be eschatological predictions. They are not concerned with others, or even with himself primarily, they are Christ centred. These are the kind of visions and revelations we need, OF THE LORD (v. 1).

147

(b) *His visions and revelations were received at a time of self effacement.* He lost consciousness of himself, so mystically was he concerned with Christ. Perhaps we should enjoy such spiritually elevating experiences if we spent less time worrying about our own advancement, and concentrated our thought and attention more upon the Person and Work of our Lord (vv. 2–3).

(c) *These visions and revelations were received when he was caught up into the paradise of God.* The Jew would refer to Paradise as the third heaven. Paradise was the word used to describe the abode of the righteous after death. Paul during these visions and revelations had for the moment anticipated the bliss of heaven. We have only to consult the letters of such a great soul as Samuel Rutherford to realise that this is possible for everyone of us, if only we are prepared to comply with the conditions.

(d) *These visions and revelations were accompanied by a voice.* You will notice that wherever in Scripture there is a vision there is a voice too, e.g. Isa. 6.8; Ezek. 1.28; Luke 9.35; Rev. 1.10. The vision is always the prelude to the voice, and notice it is a voice which calls to service.

2. WE MUST OFTEN ACCEPT OUR INFIRMITIES AS FROM THE LORD v. 7

There has been much controversy as to Paul's thorn in the flesh. Some commentators point out that literally it means 'a stake' upon which a man could be impaled. Those who take this line see here a reference to his crucifixion with Christ (see Gal. 2.20). This view has in its favour that the phrase in verse 7 'in the flesh' may possibly be 'for the flesh'. A. Way translates it, 'like a stave driven through my flesh'. Others such as Dr. Bernard in the Expositor's Greek Testament rejects this interpretation, pointing out that when the word is used in the Septuagint (Num. 33.55, Hos. 2.8) it means merely 'a thorn', which causes a continual irritation. This has the support of verse 8, where the apostle declares that on three occasions he had prayed for this 'thorn' to be removed. Whatever may have been in the mind of the apostle when he wrote this word, certainly our crucifixion with Christ balances the ecstacy of revelation we receive from Christ, while at the same time, there is nothing which brings home to us our human frailty more, than some recurring ailment which from time to time lays us low.

There are two other points we must not fail to notice in our exposition of this passage. One is that the 'thorn', whatever it may have been, is said to be 'a messenger of Satan'. Sickness belongs to the kingdom of Satan. That is why our Lord waged war upon it in the days of His flesh. So often sickness brings with it despair and depression. If we were to stop here we should indeed succumb to despair, but Paul sounds the glorious note of the sufficiency of God's grace (v. 9). It is so often only as we experience human weakness, we know of God's power. When we are weak, then we are strong (v. 10).

3. WE MUST EVER BE READY TO OBEY THE CALL OF SERVICE AS FROM THE LORD
v. 14

We certainly must not miss noting the nature of such service.

(a) *Willing service.* Paul was ready to visit Corinth yet a third time if necessary. Many of us would have washed our hands of the church at Corinth. Not so Paul, he was willing to go yet again.

(b) *Self sacrificing service.* Paul was ready to go to Corinth at his own expense so as not to be a burden to them (vv. 14, 15).

(c) *Selfless service.* He was ready to visit Corinth not for his honour, not that anyone might praise him for his fidelity to the churches he had been instrumental in founding, but for their sakes (v. 14).

(d) *Love motivated service* (v. 15). Service which is not motivated by love can become drudgery.

2 CORINTHIANS 12. 17–21

Taking Care

Here too in these closing verses of the twelfth chapter, Paul defends himself against his accusers. They declared that the apostle had derived financial gain from the visit of Titus to the city (vv. 17–18). They also said that he was excusing himself for the action he had taken, thus admitting that he had acted wrongly (v. 19). None of these accusations had a thread of truth in them. He frankly expressed his fear that when eventually he was able to visit Corinth he would find them unrepentant. It would be a humbling experience for him (v. 21), since it would mean that both his correspondence with them, and Titus' visit to them would have been in vain. He declares however that if such is the case, he will not spare them, but will deal severely with their sin (13.2). How plainly this reminds us that we must act wisely as Christians!

1. WE MUST BE CAREFUL IN OUR WALK v. 18

In verse 18 the verb 'walked' occurs twice in our English version, although it only occurs once in the original. None the less it is an important New Testament word, which is employed to describe the Christian life. John was very fond of it (1 John 1.6, 7; 2.6). It is a very apt word.

(a) *It is often possible to tell a man's trade or profession by his walk.* The sailor walks with a characteristic 'roll' which probably is the result of keeping balance on the heaving and rolling deck of a ship. The soldier moves smartly with precision, indicating that he has been drilled upon the parade ground. The policeman moves with a measured step and slow. Others should recognise us as Christians by the way in which we walk.

(b) *It is often possible to tell a man's conduct by his walk.* There is no mistaking the unsteady walk of a drunkard. There is no mistaking the movement of the criminal. He is marked by his slow soft shuffle or his quick dash to remain unseen. When we walk in the light we have nothing to hide, we can walk steadily and surely, with no fear of others.

(c) *It is often possible to tell a man's state of health from his walk.* The man who is suffering from creeping paralysis begins to shuffle. The young man enjoying health and strength will walk briskly, while the old man will walk slowly with bowed head and shoulders. Our spiritual health is often reflected in our spiritual walk.

2. *WE MUST BE CAREFUL IN OUR WORDS*
v. 19

Here we have the words 'we speak'. We cannot avoid speaking, no matter how shy and reticent we may be. Notice how we must speak as Christians:

(a) *Before God.* We must never forget that there is an ear open which hears every conversation, and notes every idle word. God is indeed the 'Unseen Guest' at every meal, who hears all we say. So often it is gossip which ruins the fellowship of a church.

(b) *In Christ.* If we bore this in mind constantly, then we should not be guilty of speaking the wrong words and engaging in idle gossip. As we are ensphered in Christ, so we must talk as those who are 'in Christ'.

(c) *For your edifying.* Paul was most concerned to build up the Christians in Corinth, especially to promote fellowship among them. Wrong words break down fellowship, the right word will build it up. This is the kind of edifying conversation we need to cultivate.

3. *WE MUST BE CAREFUL IN OUR WRATH*
v. 20

There is such a thing as righteous indignation. Our Lord displayed His wrath when he cleansed the Temple. The Revelation even refers to the 'wrath of the Lamb'. Amos was angry at the way the rich subjected the poor in his day. Paul was angry at the divisions which frustrated the work of God in Corinth. Anger however is something that must ever be subjected to the most careful scrutiny. So often what we call righteous indignation is personal pique of the most unrighteous kind.

A Proof of Christ

In this passage Paul is still concerned with the Corinthian troubles. The warning which commences in the previous chapter is continued. A third visit to the city would certainly mean a confrontation of Paul and his accusers before witnesses, in a legal manner (v. 1). The apostle felt that the evil in the church at Corinth could be tolerated no longer (v. 2). Paul was not the man to compromise where principle was concerned, or where evil was being openly practised. There are times when we must take our stand against evil and defend our principles, but we must always be sure that we are taking a stand which Christ Himself would take, and that when we speak we are speaking with Divine authority. Our opponents will require 'a proof of Christ' (v. 3) in us. They are justified in so doing. What constitutes such a proof?

1. *AN EXPRESSION OF POWER IN US*

The church at Corinth was willing and ready to recognise Christ's power among them. It had been demonstrated in Paul's preaching and in the sequel to his ministry. It was demonstrated too in the wide variety of gifts which the church at Corinth displayed. Paul wisely refers his readers to the demonstration of Christ's power. Mark what he writes concerning it,

(*a*) *Christ is ready to demonstrate His power in the church at Corinth.* A. Way translates verse 3b, 'He is not weak in His relations to you; nay, He is ready to put forth His might in your midst.' The proof of Christ's presence is His power. Where He is present then miracles of grace are performed. As Christ had demonstrated His power among them in the past, He was ready so to do at that very time. It was patent that Christ was working through Paul, his words therefore could not be without power (v. 3). Others cannot afford to ignore what we say if God's power is being demonstrated in our lives.

(*b*) *Though Christ had subjected Himself to human weakness, yet He now lives by the power of God.* It was God who worked through

152

Christ in the days of His flesh. It was God who had raised Him by His power from the dead. It is God who now channels His power into Christ for us. If Christ could not live apart from God's power, neither can we. Again, the display of Divine power enables us to speak with authority.

(c) *By reason of our union with Christ, we share both His human weakness and His Divine power.* In His humanity He shared our weakness, but in His present ministry He shares His risen power with us. If we are to offer proof to the world that we are Christ's, there is no more effective way than by giving evidence of His risen life in us.

2. *A SELF EXAMINATION BY US* v. 5

Paul called upon the church at Corinth to examine itself. Self examination is something we are reluctant to undertake. We prefer to hide our real selves under the cloak of self esteem. We are not really in a position to judge one another on many issues. As we come to the Lord's Table we are to examine ourselves. The Lord leaves the responsibility to us. If we fail to examine ourselves now, then we can be sure He will examine us at His judgement seat. Notice the character this self examination must take.

(a) *We must see whether we are really in the Faith*, or as A. Way translates it, 'holding to the faith'. It is easy to make a profession of faith, but proof demands not profession but possession of faith. Faith is something subjective that is in us, 'The Faith' is something objective which we are in. By faith we are in the Faith, that which was once delivered to the saints, and passed down to us as a precious heritage, which all who are in Christ enjoy.

(b) *We must rigorously test ourselves to the extent that our examination yields a result*. This is literally what the original means in verse 5. If Christ means to us all that we claim, then we shall readily detect both His presence and power in our lives. If however we have to search long and hard before we discover that there is anything distinctively Christian about us, then we may doubt whether we are really in the Faith. We must test so as to procure results.

(c) *We should test ourselves so that our examination not only convinces us, but convinces others*. Mark the word 'approved' in verse 7. Paul was not concerned about his approval, but rather their approval as a result of the honest inquiry into their own lives. The word in the original is that often used by a silversmith. A piece of work which did not meet with his approval was 'reprobate', *adokimos*, unapproved, while that which reached his ideal of craftmanship was *dokimos*, approved. Only such articles could be put on display for sale. Can we be displayed as those who have been fashioned by the hand of God?

3. *A PROGRESSIVE PERFECTING OF US* v. 9

Paul was so selfless that he did not concern himself in this instance with his own spiritual state, but rather with theirs. He would indeed have been weak if he had been forced to deal with the evils of Corinth by punishment. He wanted them to be strong enough to acknowledge their wrong, and right it. It is as we examine ourselves, bringing ourselves into the light of God's presence we are perfected in the Christian life.

2 CORINTHIANS 13. 11–14

A Full and Final Word

The closing verses of this epistle are in marked contrast to those which precede them. There is no sharp rebuke, no threat of judgment. It is noticeable that the apostle refers to the Corinthian believers as 'brethren'. Whatever may have been their spiritual state, however great the differences between the apostle and the church in Corinth, those in Christ were his brethren. They owned the same Father, they were born of the same Spirit. They belonged to the same family. This is something we need to bear constantly in mind. Though others differ from us, they are our 'brethren'. Like Paul we can wish them well, as we take our leave of them after some meeting with them. What a different spirit would pervade our church meetings if this were the case. Notice that in these closing verses, there are three features we must not miss.

1. AN APOSTOLIC PRECEPT v. 11a

The precept takes the form of an imperative for the sake of emphasis. What follows from the apostle's pen are not suggestions we can consider, if we wish, but injunctions that must be obeyed. How vital they are.

(a) *Be complete.* This is what is meant by 'perfect'. There cannot be perfection on earth, but we can be complete in Christ since there is all in Christ that we need. Often we see buildings which have been left unfinished for some reason or other. What a sorry spectacle they present! How often Christians present the same sorry spectacle! Unfinished!

(b) *Be strong.* In verse 9 he stated that their strength brought joy to his heart. A parent rejoices to see its child enjoying physical strength. We cannot rejoice in weakness. We are called upon to be soldiers. It is vital that a soldier is strong in the Lord of Hosts. It is necessary that in the battle of life we stand strong against the enemies of our souls. The word 'comfort' as we have seen conveys the idea of strength, it really means strengthened together. This means we must:

(c) *Be united.* 'Be of one mind.' That does not mean of course, that we are all to think alike. This is patently impossible, but it does mean we should share the same outlook, we should have a unity of purpose. Then we are bound to 'pull together'. Hitherto in Corinth they had been anything but united, consequently the progress of the church was hindered.

(d) *Be amicable.* 'Live in peace.' How necessary was this injunction to the Christians in Corinth! It is still as necessary as ever. How often we find churches torn by strife! We expect to find strife in the world but not in the church. How can we preach a message of peace to a war torn world, if we are not living in peace ourselves.

1. AN APOSTOLIC PROMISE v. 11b

'The God of love and peace shall be with you.' Of course God never forsakes us, but Paul does not merely write, 'God shall be with you'. The apostle describes God as the God 'of love and peace'. This is particularly significant in view of his injunctions in

155

the former section of the verse. God can be present, yet we do not perceive His presence. We certainly cannot see Him, where there is hatred and disquiet. Our eyes are blinded in such conditions. This is a conditional promise, a precious promise indeed.

(a) *A promise which assures us of an atmosphere of love and peace.* So infrequently has this been experienced by communities in history, it seems remote and idealistic beyond our realisation. Where the love of Christ is shed abroad in the heart and the peace which passeth all understanding is experienced, then the God of love and peace is present indeed, and His presence realised.

(b) *A promise which can be trusted.* Like so many other promises in scripture the apostle writes 'shall', not 'may', or 'perhaps will'. When we comply with the conditions, we can be sure of the consequences.

(c) *A promise which is most intimate.* 'With you.' This was an intensely personal word with which Paul closes the epistle. Love and peace are not impersonal qualities. They are conveyed from one to another. They originate in God and come to us through Christ, but they are to be passed on to others by us.

(d) *A promise which is demonstrated by one Christian to another.* This surely is implied in the 'holy kiss' and the salutation of the saints. The kiss is the sign of reconciliation and affection. It is the symbol of love, while the salutation is the evidence of peace. Love and peace must be demonstrated in action, not merely discussed in word.

3. *AN APOSTOLIC PRAYER* v. 14

The apostle concludes this epistle with what we call the benediction. It is a lovely prayer:

(a) *For grace.* 'The grace of the Lord Jesus Christ.' God's grace to us sinners was manifested in Christ, and conveyed to us through Him. We need daily grace to live for Him.

(b) *For the love of God.* We need this love shed abroad in our hearts by the Holy Spirit. We are loveless apart from Divine love implanted within.

(c) *For the communion of the Holy Ghost.* It is the Spirit of God which brings us together. Our fellowship is through the Holy Spirit.

Books suggested for further study

WM. BARCLAY, *1 and 2 Corinthians* (*Daily Study Bible*) (St. Andrews Press)

R. E. DAVIES, *Studies in 1 Corinthians* (Epworth Press)

JEAN HERING, *The First Epistle of Paul to the Corinthians* (Epworth Press)

JEAN HERING, *The Second Epistle to the Corinthians* (Epworth Press)

Layman's Commentaries on the Bible: 1 and 2 Corinthians (S.C.M. Press)

G. CAMPBELL MORGAN, *The Corinthian Letters of Paul* (Fleming H. Revell)

LEON MORRIS, *The First Epistle of Paul to the Corinthians* (*Tyndale New Testament Commentaries*) (Tyndale Press)

H. J. OCKENGA, *The Comfort of God* (Fleming H. Revell)

A. REDPATH, *Blessings out of Buffetings* (*Studies in 2 Corinthians*) (Pickering and Inglis)

R. V. G. TASKER, *The Second Epistle of Paul to the Corinthians* (*Tyndale New Testament Commentaries*) (Tyndale Press)

MARGARET E. THRALL, *1 and 2 Corinthians The Cambridge Commentary* (Cambridge University Press)